PRIDE AND PREJUDICES

PRIDE AND PREJUDICES

QUEER LIVES AND THE LAW

KEIO YOSHIDA

SCRIBE

Melbourne | London | Minneapolis

Scribe Publications
18–20 Edward St, Brunswick, Victoria 3056, Australia
2 John St, Clerkenwell, London, WC1N 2ES, United Kingdom
3754 Pleasant Ave, Suite 223w, Minneapolis, Minnesota 55409, USA

Published by Scribe 2025

Copyright © Keio Yoshida 2025

All rights reserved. Without limiting the rights under copyright reserved above, no part of this publication may be reproduced, stored in or introduced into a retrieval system, or transmitted, in any form or by any means (electronic, mechanical, photocopying, recording or otherwise) without the prior written permission of the publishers of this book.

The moral rights of the author have been asserted.

Typeset in Garamond Premier Pro by the publishers

Printed and bound in the UK by CPI Group (UK) Ltd, Croydon CR0 4YY

Scribe is committed to the sustainable use of natural resources and the use of paper products made responsibly from those resources.

978 1 761380 94 5 (Australian edition)
978 1 915590 75 6 (UK edition)
978 1 761386 33 6 (ebook)

Catalogue records for this book are available from the National Library of Australia and the British Library.

scribepublications.com.au
scribepublications.co.uk
scribepublications.com

Contents

A Note from the Author on Language	1
A Note on Privacy	3
Prologue	5
1. In Private	13
2. Are You Ready for Love?	39
3. Express Yourself	65
4. I Know a Place	97
5. Husbands and Wives	115
6. You're Having My Baby	149
7. Born This Way	177
8. I Am What I Am	203
Conclusion	231
Acknowledgements	235
Notes	237

Gay Is the Word
A Note from the Author on Language

Language is important and it is also constantly shifting. It varies between generations, and across cultures and continents. I have tried my best to be sensitive to this, but at times I use terms that are antiquated or offensive. Often this is because they are technical legal terms as set out in legislation or legal judgments. Terms such as 'sodomy', 'buggery', and 'homosexuality' are still used in legal systems around the world. This is a direct result of the legacy of British colonialism. It is important to reflect this history and reality.

In this book, I refer to lesbian, gay, bisexual, trans, and queer (LGBTQ+) rights and I also use the word 'queer'. In international human-rights law, the term 'sexual orientation and gender identity' (SOGI) is used. I also use 'intersex' when specifically referring to cases about the rights of intersex people.

Although there are differences between the terms, I use 'queer' and 'LGBTQ+' pretty much interchangeably and in the colloquial sense of my community in London: that is, 'long live queer spaces', 'I am queer', and 'queer as in fuck you'. The term 'queer' historically carried social stigma. But it is increasingly used to celebrate everyone in the LGBTQ+ community. bell hooks, the Black feminist scholar explained it in this way: 'queer not as being about who you're having sex with (that can be a dimension of it); but queer as being about the self that is at odds with everything around it and has to invent and create and find a place to speak and to thrive and to live.' Queer as a struggle against patriarchy, homophobia, racism, and coloniality as interrelated frameworks of oppression.

I refer to myself in this book as gay, lesbian, queer, genderqueer, non-binary, trans. To paraphrase Eve Kosofsky Sedgwick, I refuse to signify monolithically. For some people, these identities are exclusive, while for others we move through the world, as yet undecided on our gender journeys and exploring the joys of queer liminality. For me, 'queer' is and continues to be the best shorthand way to describe myself and the broader struggle of everyone under the rainbow umbrella. I also use various terms for myself depending on when the event took place in my life.

A Note on Privacy

I am extremely grateful to those who have given me permission to tell their stories. In some cases, I use real names; in others, the names and certain elements of the story have been changed in order to maintain people's privacy.

Finally, the views expressed in this book are my own and do not constitute legal advice.

Prologue

In July 2023, I went home to Ireland for the summer. From Ballycastle, I went to Belfast and took the train down to Dublin. I had lived in Dublin for three years as a student and am called to the Bar of Ireland, meaning that I am a barrister both in England and Wales, where I have mainly practised, and in the Republic of Ireland. I am the kind of lawyer that wears a wig and a gown and who goes to court.

I was there that time for the weekend, not for work or study but to act as a tour guide for an American friend who was visiting Ireland for the first time. Despite my years living in Ireland's capital city, to my shame I had never been to the main tourist attractions: the Guinness factory, Kilmainham Gaol, the National Gallery of Ireland — the list went on. But there's a first time for everything and I enlisted my friend Luke, a Dubliner, to help me in my task.

My first port of call was Trinity College Dublin, founded by Queen Elizabeth I in 1592, back when Ireland was under English rule. It's where I studied Irish law and French law in a class of eight (out of 120 law students). We were the biggest nerds, who wanted not only an education in common law, but an education that embraces the comparative legal traditions of the civil law too. At Trinity, with Luke and my American friend, I headed straight for the Old Library, which holds the Book of Kells, a ninth-century gospel manuscript, and the Long Room library, an impressive two-storey vista of rows upon rows of bookshelves. As we walked around the college, I showed my friends some other very important landmarks, such as the Pavilion, where I used to drink cans of cheap cider on Friday evenings before heading to the Palace nightclub, the Burke library, where I spent most of my three years, and my student residence, where I spent time with my first girlfriends, breaking hearts and getting my heart broken.

Next, the three of us headed for Merrion Square, where Luke has arranged a private guided tour of no. 1, formerly the childhood home of Oscar Wilde and now a museum. As well as being one of Ireland's most treasured writers, poets, and playwrights, Wilde is also one of Trinity's most famous alumni. After leaving Dublin, he became a fabulous celebrity in London, where he lived a flamboyant, champagne-filled lifestyle.

Oscar Wilde had been on my mind the last few years, as I wrote my book with Jen Robinson on the impact of defamation laws on people's lives. Wilde's libel trial is one of the most famous in English history. Back in 1895, when the trial took place, defamation was a criminal offence. Wilde decided to sue the Marquess of Queensbury for defamation after the aristocrat left a note at a private members' club addressed 'For Oscar Wilde, posing as a sodomite' (he spelt this word slightly wrongly). As the tour guide told us, although Wilde was married to a woman with whom he had two children, he was also having sexual liaisons with young men, including a relationship with the Marquess of Queensbury's son: Lord Alfred Douglas, nicknamed Bosie. Bosie was a poet and also a charlatan who would persuade Wilde to sue his father, a disastrous course of action.

The Marquess instructed Edward Carson QC as his barrister, a formidable lawyer who later became the attorney-general and the solicitor-general. Born in the same year, Wilde and Carson had played together as children in Dublin and became rivals or, according to some, 'sworn enemies' at Trinity College. Carson set out to defend the Marquess of Queensbury by proving that Oscar Wilde was a sodomite. In other words, that the defamatory statement was true, a defence to the libel action.

Wilde assured his lawyer, Sir Edward Clarke QC, that there was no truth whatsoever in the allegations that he was a homosexual. But Carson told the court in his opening speech that he would call to the witness stand numerous young men to give evidence about Wilde's sex life. After some days, Sir Edward urged Wilde to withdraw his libel charge against the Marquess. He knew that the prosecution for libel would fail and that Wilde's reputation would be destroyed by the evidence that would be presented. The risk was not simply that losing the libel trial would ruin Wilde's reputation and that he would have to pay expensive legal costs, but that being gay was a crime. In England, gay men were prosecuted under different criminal laws. Henry VIII had criminalised gay sex for the first time under the *Buggery Act 1533*. This law carried the potential of a death sentence, and gay men were executed until 1835 under this law.

The hostile environment against gay men continued and, ten years before Wilde's trial, parliament extended the list of acts that were criminalised with the *Criminal Law Amendment Act 1885*. Section 11 of this amendment, also known as the Labouchere Amendment after the member of parliament who proposed it, criminalised 'gross indecency' between consenting men, even in private, and gay men could be prosecuted on the basis of affectionate correspondence. This law meant that it was no longer only anal sex that was criminalised, but broader sex acts between men. The ambiguous wording of the crime of gross indecency meant that the laws were referred to as the 'Blackmailer's Charter'. People were policed on the basis of suspicion and on the basis of their appearance. The scope of the law was impossibly wide, and prosecutors had a much easier time of proving gross indecency than the offence of buggery.

In the 1950s, the Wolfenden Committee, which wrote the report recommending the decriminalisation of homosexuality in England and Wales, was set up by the Conservative government due to the authorities' fears that the laws could be used against gay members of the civil service to blackmail them into giving state secrets to the Soviet Union. Decriminalisation of homosexuality was not considered because of an understanding that gay people have equal rights to love and form intimate relationships with whom they choose. The Committee's report was good news for gay men, but it led to a travesty of justice for women, with the Committee recommending the criminalisation of street prostitution. The *Street Offences Act 1959* made it a crime to be a 'common prostitute', a gender-specific crime and one that remains today in a different form.

Back in April 1895, Wilde was in serious trouble for his actions. Three days after he withdrew the libel case against his lover's father, a warrant was issued for his arrest and he was brought before Bow Street Magistrates' Court to face charges relating to his homosexuality.

Wilde was put on trial at the Old Bailey, the grand criminal court in London. Sir Edward Clarke would represent him once again, this time acting for free as a defence lawyer. The trial resulted in a hung jury, meaning that they couldn't reach a verdict and Wilde had to go through a criminal trial once again. In the second trial, Wilde was convicted of numerous counts of gross indecency and sentenced to two years in prison with hard labour in Reading Gaol, the harshest imprisonment that the judge could mete out under the law. The trials would later bankrupt Wilde. His prison sentence also broke his heart, as Wilde remained in love with Bosie but heard from him less and less frequently.

We sat in the front room of the museum, three queer people, and listened as the guide told us how after Wilde's conviction, he was forced to stand in handcuffs and prison clothes on the train platform at Clapham Junction on his way to Reading Gaol. During the 30 minutes in which he waited on the platform, Wilde was subjected to horrific homophobic abuse — jeered at, spat at, under conditions of 'unspeakable humiliation'. Traumatised, Wilde would cry every year on the anniversary of the incident for the rest of his life. Beside me, my two friends also shed a tear, sitting in his childhood home.

In prison, Wilde's suffering continued. His mother, who he loved deeply, died while he was in prison, and he was unable to attend her funeral. He was taken to the Bankruptcy Court twice, and according to his writing in *De Profundis*, his children were removed from his care after it was decided that he was unfit to be with them, 'a blow so appalling that I did not know what to do'. After his release from prison, Wilde did not recover and lived in exile in France. He died penniless and ruined in a bedsit in Paris in 1900. He is often referred to as a gay martyr. There was no redemption for him.

After the tour, the three of us blinked our way into the Dublin sunshine to wander around Merrion Square in an Ireland that had repealed the legislation outlawing homosexuality in the 1990s. It is startling that, in only a few decades, Ireland has become a vanguard of LGBTQ+ rights — the first country in the world to hold a referendum in favour of gay marriage in 2015, and one of the first countries to pass a gender-recognition law allowing trans people to self-declare their gender. It has even had an openly gay head of government. A very different Ireland to the one in which Wilde grew up, and even where I grew up. It is a real example of how change can happen.

There are places where the law that ruined Wilde's life — or versions of it — remain in place. Queer people continue to be blackmailed, arrested, prosecuted, criminalised, humiliated, rejected by their families, persecuted by country and society, and in some cases faced with the death penalty. The experience of Wilde — prosecuted, subject to humiliation in the press, publicly shamed, and incarcerated — is unfortunately not one which is consigned to the history books. Queer people around the world are subject to these human-rights violations simply for loving and being who they are.

This book is about the ongoing battle for LGBTQ+ rights and the right to live our authentic queer lives. It's about how far we have come, and how far we have to go, with a focus on the way the law can both oppress us and liberate us from human-rights violations. It is about the need to secure a right to authentic queer life so that we can march, sing, dance, hold hands, kiss, make love, make families, have careers, access the healthcare we need, wear the clothes we want to wear, cut our hair — in short, do all the mundane, everyday things and all the extraordinary, joyful things that make queer life what it is. It is about our right to live our best queer lives free of state oppression and to love. It is about all the things that Wilde and so many people have been denied due to state and societal homophobia. It is about the desire for a better and more equitable world.

This is a book about queer lives, my life, and how the law continues to impact, regulate, and punish lesbian, gay, bisexual, trans, queer, and intersex lives. In this book, I set out some of the major battles LGBTQ+ people face around the world today and argue that we must strengthen legal protections. From the battles to protect queer bars and spaces and hold pride marches, to outlawing conversion therapy and overturning laws that criminalise same-sex intimacy and require trans sterilisation, the fight is far from over. This is particularly true when it comes to the rights of trans, intersex, and gender-nonconforming people. It is shocking that international and regional human-rights courts still deny intersex people the right to identify as such on their birth certificates, or that laws require trans men to be registered as mothers. Often the rules simply don't make sense. They are heterosexual and heterosexist legal fictions. This book outlines case law (decisions by courts) from around the world to illustrate the different legal problems we continue to have whether we are simply trying to get on with our lives or trying to enact revolution.

In this book, I argue that the law must move from a place of non-discrimination to positive affirmation. I want us to imagine what the world might look like if the law provided us with a right to be here and be queer. I want us to imagine how such legal affirmation — on our own terms, not in comparison with heterosexuality — might give us a different vision for a queer future. In this book, I want to carry out a queer manifestation. A manifestation for authentic queer lives in law and life.

A fabulous, joyous queer authentic life.

Chapter 1
In Private

In 1998, I was 13 years old and living in Holywood, Northern Ireland. Famous for its Maypole and golf. It was the year of the Good Friday Agreement, a treaty that ended the Troubles and brought peace in the North after years of conflict in a territory that sits in the island of Ireland but politically and legally remains part of the United Kingdom. It was also the year that George Michael was arrested in a Beverly Hills restroom by an undercover police officer. Shortly after his release, he laughed off the incident on a late-night chat show: I'll show you mine, you show me yours, and then the police officer arrests you. The pop star later released an iconic single, 'Outside'. A camp re-enactment of the incident where he dresses up as an LA police officer and dances in front of glittering urinals. I didn't understand why he was arrested and entrapped in this way.

My first kiss was with a girl in a tree-house two years

later. It was 2000. I was 15 years old, or perhaps I had just turned 16. She was a popular girl in school, just my type. Smart, blonde, brave, and feminine. She dressed like Britney Spears in low-slung ripped jeans and had a belly-button piercing. I couldn't tell anybody about my first kiss, so I wrote about it in my diary in terms that I thought might be cryptic. I'm pretty sure I used some mathematical symbols and Greek characters, even though I was terrible at maths and certainly didn't speak Greek. I learnt these from my girl crush, who was somehow aware of Pi and Theta. I didn't write many specific details about my crush. I didn't write about how I wanted to touch her face, her skin, her thighs and to lie in her bed kissing all night. I didn't write about how I liked to watch her dance or how I thought she was smarter than me and much more popular. I didn't write about how I would read poetry and think about her. I just wrote down that we kissed in her back garden in a tree-house. It was pitch black outside and we had stolen some of her mother's cheap New Zealand wine. I had somehow procured a cigarette from somewhere. We talked about the school talent-show dance troupe she was leading, and I talked about the Vietnam War, which we were studying in history class together. We talked and our bodies moved closer together, until our lips collided. I knew that I wasn't meant to kiss girls, but I had no idea it would feel so good. It felt so right.

I wrote about it in the diary because I couldn't tell anybody. She had a boyfriend, and he was older and nice. Also, nobody would voluntarily talk about being gay. Being gay was a bad thing. An insult. *That's so gay.* We both knew instinctively that this was our secret. Something that might be normal in a friendship between teenage girls, or something that maybe wasn't so normal. We weren't sure. How would we know? The internet was only just coming into our homes, but there was no social media or search engines to turn to. Girls certainly did not kiss each other in the novels I took out from the school library. It would take another five years until I would get my hands on *Oranges Are Not the Only Fruit*. The only information available was in the form of rumours about who was gay in town and the clear religious dictates on what we should not be doing: no drinking, no getting into cars with boys, no sex, no being gay.

Not long after I'd written the entry, my mother found and read my diary. I was asked to come downstairs from my bedroom and taken into the drawing room, the good room full of aspirations and judgment reserved for special guests and moral interventions. It was meticulously decorated in classic English style. Laura Ashley, floral curtains. It was in this setting that my mother sat me down in such a way that I knew I was in trouble. She questioned me about my crush. I felt deeply ashamed. Perverted. Wrong.

Following the extraction of my confession — which wasn't difficult, since I had written the facts in my diary — I was banned from seeing my girl crush again, in her house or in mine. Sleepovers, with her or anyone else, were now strictly out of the question. I was completely devastated. On her 18th birthday, three years later, my mother allowed me to go to the party, an hour away, on the condition that I drive up and back on the same night. I drove through the fog with Celine Dion's version of 'I Drove All Night' on repeat, wild with teenage angst. I ached for years at the loss. It was the first time that I had my heart broken, and it wasn't because a girl broke up with me but because it was prohibited. It was because in my house at that time queer love was, in the words of Bosie's poem to Oscar Wilde, a love that dare not speak its name.

I saw her at school, of course, where we would pass each other in corridors, in our regulation uniforms with skirts worn too short. I would even sit beside her in history class, where I could smell her sweet cheap perfume and would ache to reach out and touch her. Even to brush my knee against hers. A few months after my mother's discovery of the kiss, I couldn't stand it anymore. I decided I had to ghost her. I had to cut contact with my best friend, not because I hated her, but because of the exact opposite. I realised this was more than a friendship, that I loved her. Or at least, I wanted to love a girl and I wanted a girl to love me back. I didn't even have time to ask her if she had feelings for me.

There was no one I could speak to about my heartache. I didn't know anybody who was gay or out. I was so confused. The kiss had felt so beautiful and my feelings felt pure. But I was being told that I was wrong, that it was wrong. Gay people were marginalised, laughed at. Being gay meant being an outcast. Some gay men were visible as hairdressers or Elton John, but I can't recall seeing or hearing about a single lesbian, other than it being an insult. I was alone and felt completely helpless and alienated. Late one night, out in my own garden, I destroyed the diary in a symbolic act of immolation. Robbed of my first love, I burnt not only my words but her letters to me. My poems to her. Birthday cards that said nothing inappropriate but had her name signed with a heart beside it. A black-and-white Polaroid of the two of us smiling. It all went up in flames.

In an attempt to correct my teenage transgressions, I was sent to a youth group at St Colmcille's church on Tuesday evenings. On the chapel floor, teenage bodies lay spread out, while a semi-modern sound system played 'Everybody Hurts' by REM. My mind has wiped the details of those weekly sessions from my memory. Who led them — was it the priests? Teenage bodies lying in the round like some die-in protest in the dark. What was the purpose of it all? I lay on the ground and thought about my own hurt; I was terrified about my future — what if the world was going to be a sad and lonely place for me? Would I be able to have a family? Would I be loved?

At the time, it hardly seemed strange that I should find myself lying on a church floor. At school, people spoke in tongues. Once, some Canadian young adults came to talk to us about abstinence. They had a paper heart and ripped it into tiny pieces. Adam has sex, heart rips, then he has sex again, heart rips, until his heart is broken into pieces. The sixth-form students giggled nervously. What if Adam were queer, I thought? Would his heart be broken in the same way? But the Canadians did not mention gay sex at all.

I consider my mother's reading of my diary, the privacy invasion, my first attempt to come out. My mother could not comprehend it. She believed that I was departing from heterosexuality as a form of rebellion. Tall, blonde, and intelligent, with sharp blue eyes and her heart full of love, she could only imagine me being safe and happy as a straight person. She wanted me to marry a good boy, to fit into society. She was trying to 'protect me' from a phase.

Her way of doing this was devastating for me. Hands shaking, she suggested to me that my kiss might have criminal implications. Could a kiss between two girls really be a crime? I watched the George Michael video on TV and didn't understand why he had been arrested. Was it because he was gay? I would later learn that it was never a crime for women to kiss in Northern Ireland, but I didn't know that then, and I'm pretty sure my mother did not know it either. I was terrified. I was under strict surveillance now. My movements closely monitored by my mother, who was equally terrified that her 'eldest daughter' might be a lesbian. I went deep into the closet while I mourned my lost chance at exploring love.

My little queer self should have been openly discussing my new crush, and the ups and downs of experiencing love for the first time. Instead, I felt despair. I didn't understand then the difference between a crime and a sin. Why was it that a kiss between girlfriends was taboo in my house while my mother happily chatted to my younger sister about her boyfriend? My sister was even allowed to go away with her boyfriend and his family to a caravan in Donegal. Like many young queer teenagers, I decided to keep my desire a secret. I went to house parties. I kissed a few boys to make sure my school friends would not suspect that I liked girls. I wore my hair long. I passed as straight. I even tried to convince myself that I could be straight, though I couldn't manage to fancy any of the boys. I wasn't ready to come out as queer. I didn't know how happy I would become and how much society would change in such a short space of time.

I didn't know it then, but journalling love crimes, like I had done as a teenager in Holywood, was how Jeffrey Dudgeon, a 35-year-old shipping clerk from Belfast, ended up setting one of the most important global legal precedents for LGBTQ+ rights in the 1980s. Gay sex was mainly decriminalised in England and Wales in 1967, but not in Northern Ireland or Scotland, the other parts of the United Kingdom. The different parts of the UK had to battle separately to decriminalise homosexuality, as with the more recent battles to decriminalise abortion (which remain ongoing).

When Dudgeon was a teenager in 1970s Belfast — about a 15-minute drive from Holywood — the Troubles were raging. In a bid to prevent decriminalisation extending to Northern Ireland, the Reverend Ian Paisley (imagine a fire-and-brimstone older version of Trump with a Belfast accent) was running his infamous campaign to 'Save Ulster from Sodomy'. This would remain a slogan in the 1980s, when I was born, and the Reverend Ian Paisley would remain the leader of the Democratic Unionist Party (DUP) until 2008, my last year at university.

Back in the 1970s, at the same time as Paisley's campaign, but on the other side of the political divide, Catholic bishops were arguing that proposals to decriminalise homosexuality in the province would 'lead to a further decline in moral standards and to a climate of moral laxity which would endanger and put undesirable pressures on those most vulnerable, namely the young'. The

Catholics and the Protestants seemed to be united by only one thing — that gays and abortions were not to be tolerated. However, it wasn't only religious groups that opposed liberalisation, but also senior members of the judiciary.

In Jeffrey Dudgeon's time, the laws remained the same as those that affected Oscar Wilde. A person prosecuted for the crime of gay sex in Northern Ireland faced a maximum sentence of life imprisonment for 'buggery'. The laws also criminalised 'gross indecency', which had no specific definition but was understood to relate to any acts of intimacy between men. You didn't even need to give or receive a blow job — an attempt to commit an offence was an offence itself. The police would use these laws to raid homes and drag gay men out of their bedrooms, as well as set up surveillance units to monitor the movements of gay men.

On 21 January 1976, Dudgeon's house was raided by the police. The Royal Ulster Constabulary (RUC), as it was called at the time, went through all his belongings and read his letters, diaries, and personal papers, which included mention of gay sex. It was this that led to his arrest. Although he was not prosecuted in the end, journalling his love crimes like I had decades later led him into hot legal water. I understand a man's impulse to write about love, sex, desire, and longing in a diary. To detail our worlds, which were and are still so absent from literature, film, and culture. The 'desire to show you to everyone I love', as the poet Adrienne Rich has written. Rather than the surveillance of my mother, Jeffrey Dudgeon had his privacy violated in the most horrendous way by the footmen of the state, entering his house, his bedroom, and policing his life choices. The police searched everything, read his diaries, and looked through his bins, apparently even fishing out an apple core to enter into evidence. Original sin.

At 35 years old, Dudgeon decided that something had to be done about the injustice he faced that night when the police raided his home. He built a nearly all-gay legal team that included the English barrister Terry Munyard. I was introduced to Terry at a party in his barrister's chambers in 2016. Terry is a man with a twinkle in his eye. He knew from his own lived experience how the law could be used to police and destroy the lives of gay men even in England. While he was active for the Campaign for Homosexual Equality in 1976, as a budding student barrister, he was arrested one night in Hyde Park. He was brought before Bow Street Magistrates' Court the next morning — 'the very court Oscar Wilde stood in'. Terry was prosecuted, went through a jury trial, and was eventually acquitted. But it made him realise how badly gay men were being treated in the criminal justice system. For a whole year Terry had had to wait for hearings to begin, and then his very being was put on trial. It was this experience that led him to fight for gay rights in the UK, set up Gay Legal Advice, and later help argue Dudgeon's case.

Instead of challenging the criminalisation of homosexuality in the national courts in Northern Ireland, Jeffrey Dudgeon and his lawyers went directly to the French city of Strasbourg, where the European Court of Human Rights (ECHR) sits. This court can make decisions on human-rights claims from member states of the Council of Europe, 46 countries in total who have signed up to the European Convention on Human Rights. I'm told the legal team road-tripped their way to France to argue the case, singing along while ABBA and Queen played on the radio and staying in the houses of gay men who would put them up for free and cheer them on in their legal journey. The trip was worth it.

The ECHR held on 22 October 1981 that the UK was violating Dudgeon's privacy rights under Article 8 of the Convention, which includes not only a right to personal privacy, but also protection against state interference into our homes and our personal correspondence. The court's decision makes it clear that countries in Europe cannot criminalise gay sex, because it breaches fundamental human rights. It was the first time that a regional or international human-rights court would rule that criminalising gay people violates our fundamental human rights. Dudgeon was on a mission to make legal history, and he succeeded, setting a precedent that continues to reverberate around courtrooms today. It should be a huge source of pride for queer people in Belfast that one of our own has made such a global impact.

The decision was also hugely significant for LGBTQ+ rights in Northern Ireland, bringing it in line with the other parts of the UK. In the year after the judgment, parliament enacted legislation to decriminalise homosexuality: the *Homosexual Offences (Northern Ireland) Order 1982*. By 1982, the whole of the UK had largely decriminalised gay sex save for a few exceptions. There was a specific exemption in the law that meant merchant seamen on ships and those in the armed forces could still be guilty of a criminal offence for having gay sex. Also, threesomes continued to be criminalised, since only sex acts between two men in private were legal (one can only imagine what the court would have said about chemsex parties). For this reason, some gay-rights activists have spoken of 'partial decriminalisation' and a 'narrow legislative win'.

Although the law changed in Northern Ireland in 1982, society was still to catch up. The RUC continued to enforce criminalisation under the guise of indecency laws. Gay men were still being surveilled, photographed, and investigated coming in and out of buildings, including for social meet-ups over cups of tea. The specific laws on homosexuality may have been repealed, but gay men were still being targeted. Gay men feared state persecution and the so-called 'pretty police'. It's hard to believe, but back in the 1980s attractive young policemen would wear tight plain clothes and target gay men coming out of nightclubs. Young men who perhaps hadn't had much luck that night would be asked if they would like to go home for some fun and find themselves arrested for the crime of 'persistent importuning' when they assented. They were baited and entrapped. My colleagues lived through this. It is not so long ago. There are so many George Michaels searching for their freedom. And in so many countries, it is the state and the police who continue to enforce society's prejudice and homophobia.

In the 1970s and 1980s, queer people were unable to come out in their workplaces due to a lack of employment discrimination protection. Gay people had little protection and my older barrister colleagues have told me how they would represent men who were fired for simply going to a gay bar. The HIV epidemic soon made prejudice against the queer community even worse. Queer people were rejected by their families and had to find spaces to meet and come together to advocate for civil rights. Enacting equality laws and non-discrimination provisions became an important part of the strategy to ensure that queer people could live their lives without widespread prejudice and violence.

This was the social context into which I was born.

Some weeks after my diary violation in Northern Ireland, I felt hopeless and tried to drink myself into oblivion. I drank a bottle of vodka in my house on a Tuesday night with my family sitting downstairs. I wanted to pass out, to numb the pain. I was 16 years old. I drank because I didn't see a path to my freedom, to queer joy, to be able to be my authentic self. I drank because I didn't know that I could be happy, could have the chance to be in love. The chance to live my life, choose my partners, be myself, write my own life script. There were no campaigns telling me that things would get better.

A few years after my first kiss and the saga that followed it, I sat in my friend Ruth's basement watching *Popstars: The Rivals*. Ruth lived in nearby Bangor. She was pretty and blonde, a cool girl in school, and had recently joined a new evangelical church. My school was full of kids who listened to Christian rock music and attended Manifest, a Christian festival. Some cried during assembly when they confessed their boring sins or told us how they had been 'saved'. In more recent years, I'm told they hold prayer circles for my former classmates who have come out. In my school years, they modelled the moral code of evangelism brought over from the US. It was cool to wear WWJD (What would Jesus do?) bracelets and make vows of chastity until marriage.

During that nondescript Saturday evening watching *Popstars* in the den of a middle-class Protestant household in County Down, Ruth told us proudly how her new church 'helped' gay people. She told us how a young man was kidnapped in a van by his own family, who drove him back 'home' and 'cured' him into 'being straight'. She told us that in her church congregation there were ex-gays and lesbians who were in a relationship together. They had prayed away the gay. I listened to this in shock and realised that I was not safe. She didn't know that I was queer. She didn't know that while she told this story I was watching Cheryl Tweedy, now Cheryl, out of the corner of my eye on the TV. Cheryl was hot. I had a calendar of Cheryl hidden in my chest of drawers wearing lingerie. I fancied Cheryl, but I didn't say that to Ruth or the schoolgirls gathered around eating pizza. I was scared I'd be ostracised. I felt like I was going to be sick.

Back then, I did not know that Ruth was talking about 'conversion therapy'. I had not seen documentaries and films such as *For the Bible Tells Me So* or *The Miseducation of Cameron Post*, which depict how religious organisations try and change a person's sexual orientation or gender identity. Conversion therapy happens all over the world and takes many different forms. According to the European Union, there are three main types of interventions: (1) psychotherapeutic interventions, including behavioural and cognitive therapy, as well as electroshocks and the use of nausea-inducing drugs, (2) medical interventions, including the administration of hormones and steroids and previously including castration and lobotomy, and (3) interventions based on religion, faith, and spirituality, which range in practice from guidance-based interventions to exorcisms.

The EU recognises these conversion practices as 'discriminatory, degrading and dehumanising, often based on homophobia' and that they violate a range of human rights of LGBTQ+ people, including the rights to privacy, dignity, integrity and personal autonomy, equality, and health, and may amount to torture, cruel, inhumane, and degrading treatment. There is a growing trend in many EU countries of banning these practices given that homosexuality (since 1990) and being trans (since 2019) are no longer considered to be pathologies by the World Health Organization. In Ireland, the government announced in 2023 that it would ban conversion therapy after the School of Nursing and Midwifery published a report detailing how a 12-year-old was illegally given electroshock treatment. Conversion practices are still legal in the UK at the time of writing.

Years after my *Popstars*-viewing days, I met a man who had gone through electroshock therapy as part of his 'conversion'. It was his religious parents who tried to 'cure' him. He was annihilated and suffers horrendous mental-health consequences today. Facing these interventions, some queer youngsters see that the only way to preserve themselves is to run away from home, to seek people who will love them for who they are; they break free even if life will be hard, and that is why so many LGBTQ+ young people still end up homeless.

I was a teenager 20 years before countries started to

legislate for bans on conversion therapies. Its unsurprising that in this context, no one came out at school. Nearly everyone — for clearly there were many of us — came out after we left. Many people ended up first in heterosexual marriages; others spent their time praying for change. This is a story that is not unique to Ireland; I have queer friends from all over the world who have similar stories or who even experienced religious interventions.

Conversion practices are ongoing. According to *Time* magazine, conversion therapy is still happening in almost every state in the US despite 26 states outlawing the practice. Conversion is mainly carried out by religious groups, and 'treatment' is provided privately, meaning that people get rich off the techniques. The United Nations has even described it as a lucrative business.

Religious groups have tried to bring court challenges to legalise the practice once again. They have argued that bans violate the right to free speech of religious therapists. In 2023, a Christian therapist in the US attempted to challenge the prohibition on licensed therapists from practising conversion therapy on children. Brian Tingley, a Washington State marriage and family counsellor wanted to argue before the US Supreme Court that the ban violates the First Amendment of the US Constitution, because it limits his free-speech rights on issues relating to sexual orientation and gender identity. He had the backing of 12 states and the Alliance Defending Freedom, a conservative Christian legal group that is influential in challenging abortion rights and LGBTQ+ rights. Thankfully, the Supreme Court refused to hear his case.

The battle to prohibit conversion therapy is an important struggle for LGBTQ+ people around the world today and one we have to advocate for. I sometimes think it's a miracle that I'm proud and queer, in a world of what Adrienne Rich calls 'compulsory heterosexuality'. Such is our capacity for survival, our innate knowledge that queer joy and love lie around the corner. That our love is beautiful and just as worthy of protection, and encouragement. Clearly there is no place for conversion therapies in our societies. Our identities and sexualities do not need to be changed, but rather respected and celebrated.

Once I turned 18, like many teenagers, I couldn't wait to leave home. I had left school and gone to Trinity with the hope that a move to the big city would provide me with greater freedom. I was right and wrong. Right because on my first day in the residential halls I met a beautiful Welsh woman, Olivia, who was studying Spanish and Italian and who would soon become my first real girlfriend. She listened to Erykah Badu, smoked rollie cigarettes, and gave me Jeannette Winterson to read. We would spend hours watching seasons of *The L Word* and subtitled films like *Todo Sobre Mi Madre*. Olivia had long blondish hair and wore a hippy head scarf. She was nothing like any stereotypes of lesbians I'd seen. She was out and easy in herself. But I didn't feel quite ready to uncover. The relationship for our first year was a secret even from our flatmates and closest friends. People just weren't really out back then. Even the hockey girls who everyone knew were gay had boyfriends.

I didn't see the ideal conditions for coming out which I thought I'd find in the big smoke of Dublin. I had thought that Trinity College would be a liberal paradise. Trinity, it turned out, was not. There were about 100 law students in my year. I can't recall a single other student being out at the time. If one in ten of us are gay, how could it be that I was the only one? When I lived down south, there was no recognition of same-sex partnerships, no same-sex marriage, and abortion was prohibited by criminal law. Ireland pre-2010 was socially conservative.

It was only when I went to law school at Trinity that I would learn about queer legal history. One of the first legal judgments I remember reading in my first year of law school was about the criminalisation of homosexuality in Ireland. It was another legacy of colonial rule by the British, who exported homophobia and life imprisonment for buggery or carnal knowledge around the world, often through what is termed Section 377. These homophobic laws were the laws of empire. It was introduced in Africa, India, East Asia, Australia, and the Pacific. Sodomy offences, buggery offences, and life imprisonment were all hallmarks of British colonial rule, which activists around the world are still trying to unpick and undo, as independent governments have since decided to uphold and even in some places strengthen the punishments meted out to the LGBTQ+ community.

In Ireland, despite independence and the enactment of its own constitution in 1937, the *Offences Against the Person Act 1861* and the *Criminal Law Amendment Act*

1885 stayed on the statute books. These laws provided that gay men convicted of buggery would receive a sentence of at least ten years and at most a life sentence. It would take David Norris, an activist and academic expert on James Joyce, 14 years of campaigning and legal challenges to change the law in Ireland.

Norris was a 38-year-old lecturer in English at Trinity College. He decided to challenge criminalisation in 1977, arguing his case through the domestic courts before reaching the Supreme Court in Dublin. Norris was a founding member of the Campaign for Homosexual Law Reform, which sought to challenge the *Offences Against the Person Act* and the *Criminal Law Amendment Act.* He wrote in his witness statement that he was shocked to find out that these laws, the same laws that ruined Oscar Wilde, were still in force in Ireland.

The court was told that Norris was 'congenitally and irreversibly homosexual in outlook and disposition'. Norris explained how he had been physically attacked, suffered from verbal abuse, and feared prosecution under the laws. He explained that the criminal laws led to a repressive and constricting environment, which meant he had to live a furtive and closeted life. Given that a human-rights court in Strasbourg had by that point in proceedings found that the same law in Northern Ireland was a violation of fundamental human rights, you would think that it was an open and shut case. If I were his lawyer, I would have told him he had a good chance of winning and overturning the criminal prohibitions on homosexuality and that the time had come since Jeffrey Dudgeon had won his case at the European Court of Human

Rights. But the Irish legal system, it turned out, was still steeped in prejudice. Norris lost in the lower courts. Saddled with thousands of pounds in legal costs, he appealed his case to the Supreme Court.

It was 22 April 1983 when the Irish Supreme Court delivered its judgment. The majority judgment was delivered by the chief justice at the time, Thomas Francis O'Higgins. O'Higgins had twice run to be president of Ireland and been twice defeated. He was appointed to the High Court and leap-frogged his way onto the Supreme Court. He had an illustrious political and legal career. The chief justice started by describing the case as a challenge to the 'criminalisation and punishment of sexual acts and conduct of a kind usually regarded and described as abnormal or unnatural'. It's not hard to see why Norris would go on to lose his case in the Supreme Court given how gay sex was being described. *Abnormal. Unnatural.* The court focused on the sex acts rather than on Norris's rights to live his life and form loving relationships.

Chief justice O'Higgins dismissed the constitutional and human-rights claims made by Norris and his legal team, that his rights to privacy and equality were being violated, on the basis that the legislature (the Dáil) was entitled to prohibit sexual conduct between men because of the 'social problem which it creates'. The Supreme Court judge opined that just because it was difficult or even harmful for a homosexual man to comply with the law, this did not mean that it was unconstitutional, since 'the exigencies of the common good must prevail'. But what common good was that? What was the social problem the court was so concerned with?

According to the Irish Supreme Court judges, the law had a legitimate aim since the criminalisation of homosexuality protects suggestible people 'from indulging in their homosexual fantasies'. He reasoned, 'there is probably a large number of people in this country with homosexual tendencies', but ...

> Of these, however, only a small number are exclusively homosexual in the sense that their orientation is congenital and irreversible. It is this small group (of those with homosexual tendencies) who must look to the others for the kind of relationship, stable or promiscuous, which they seek and desire. It follows that the efforts and activities of the congenital must tend towards involving the homosexually orientated in more and more deviant sexual acts to such an extent that such involvement may become habitual. The evidence in this case and the textbooks produced as part thereof indicate how sad, lonely and harrowing the life of a person, who is or has become exclusively homosexual, is likely to be.

The law was there to ensure that those on the straight and narrow didn't become joyful queers. That they wouldn't be manipulated and led astray by the dastardly 'congenital gays', of which the chief justice thought there were only a few — and those who were 'exclusively homosexual' were sad and lonely. He didn't ever stop to think that it might be criminalisation that makes gays sad and lonely, criminalised and policed by the state, scared that even private acts in bedrooms behind closed doors and pulled curtains might result in a raid. The chief justice's main concern was the danger posed to heterosexual marriage: if queers could celebrate their intimacy without fear of criminalisation, then everyone might turn gay. This was a judgment of heterosexual fragility.

The chief justice concluded his judgment by writing that homosexual conduct is, 'of course, morally wrong, and has been so regarded by mankind through the centuries'. He found that very serious harm is involved in homosexual conduct, even between private consenting males given that 'known devotees multiply'. In what is one of the most striking sentences of the judgment, he explained that 'Such conduct, although carried on with full consent, may lead a mildly homosexually orientated person into a way of life from which he may never recover ...' The court rejected Norris's claim without citing a single legal case in support of its opinion. All it relied upon was prejudice.

On this basis, the Supreme Court of Ireland upheld the criminalisation of gay sex in 1983. In a year when queers around the world were dancing their gay socks off to tunes such as 'I Want to Break Free', 'Flashdance', and 'Total Eclipse of the Heart', it was still a crime in Ireland to be gay.

I was 18 years old when I read the case for the first time. After I read the judgment, I wandered absolutely incensed around the law library, which we called 'The Pit', a grey brutalist basement. Back then, we still read cases in the law reports, in books with the cases ordered by year of judgment, their pages pencil-marked and annotated by the law students before us. I looked mad as I paced the library, angrily waving the book in my hand in the air at an imaginary gallery of judges past, calling their attention to the horrific injustice to Mr Norris and all the other gays living in Ireland in the 1980s and before.

I looked mad because I was mad, raging. In my first few weeks of law school, reading judgments like this placed a fire in me to take on the legal system with its sustained injustices. In Ireland when I was living there between 2004 and 2008, there was no right to an abortion, and gay marriage was not available. It was steeped in patriarchy. While others were out partying, I spent my time in the law library reading cases from around the world on LGBTQ+ rights and thinking about getting married just to take on the law. I became committed to becoming a human-rights lawyer because I was enraged by the law's complicity in denying us our fundamental human rights. In denying us the basic dignities that heterosexual people take for granted. I wanted to fight.

All these years later, and over a decade of human-rights legal practice, I am still outraged that this judgment was written by a celebrated judge who would go on to receive a judicial appointment to the European Court of Justice. A judge that upheld a law imposing penal servitude for life for those who 'indulge' in their queer fantasies was rewarded with a top legal position in the European Union. My criminal-law professor at the time, Ivana Bacik, who would influence my legal thinking by introducing me to feminist approaches to the law, described the case as 'the worst Supreme Court judgment ever'. Amen.

In the same case, Justice Niall McCarthy gave a dissenting judgment. This is an individual opinion from a judge disagreeing with the majority opinion. He would have allowed the constitutional challenge, meaning Norris would have won his case. The legal reasoning of the dissenting judge is fascinating. Why can a man masturbate on his own, or with a woman, but not two men together? McCarthy finds that this is a breach of Norris's privacy rights and the rights of gay men to sexual intimacy. However, McCarthy was all too aware that activists for abortion rights could also use the language of privacy, so he used the occasion to clarify that any extension of privacy rights to homosexuals would not extend them to women and their right to have an abortion. He was willing to grant rights to men to masturbate together but not to grant women fundamental rights to bodily autonomy.

In October 1983, months after the Supreme Court judgment in *Norris v Attorney General*, the Eighth Amendment of the Irish Constitution came into law. Following a referendum, the Irish people decided to elevate the prohibition of abortion into the constitution through this amendment. This provision enshrined the right to life of the unborn and stated that it has due regard to the equal right to life of the mother. Nineteen eighty-three was a dark year for Ireland, one which would continue to cost women their lives until another referendum repealed the Eighth Amendment in 2018. The two events in the same year show how gay rights and abortion rights are often linked — denying people their bodily autonomy, privacy, equality, dignity, and even life.

Like Jeffrey Dudgeon, David Norris brought his case to the European Court of Human Rights after he lost his case in the Irish Supreme Court. He would win there in

1988. Mary Robinson, who had been his junior counsel in the domestic courts, and later became president of Ireland, argued his case before the court in Strasbourg. The European judges explained that any 'justifications as there are for retaining the law in force unamended are outweighed by the detrimental effects which the very existence of the legislative provision in question can have on the life of a person of homosexual orientation ...' While members of the public might be 'shocked, offended or disturbed' by homosexuality, that was no reason to criminalise consenting adults from engaging in intimacy together. Even if the law was not being enforced, even if Norris had never been arrested or prosecuted, the court held that his privacy rights were being violated due to the very existence of the criminalisation of homosexual practices.

The law in the Republic of Ireland was changed in 1993, five years after the Strasbourg judgment. Ireland was one of the last countries in Western Europe to decriminalise gay sex. David Norris would go on to become Ireland's first openly gay man in public office, a senator, and would even run for president. But the fact that it took Ireland until the 1990s, when I was a young child, to decriminalise homosexuality has led to a lot of soul searching. Fintan O'Toole, one of Ireland's most famous journalists, has argued that with the HIV epidemic the judgment cost many gay men their lives.

The same laws certainly cost Oscar Wilde his.

These judgments are part of the journey in international human-rights law towards the recognition of the rights of LGBTQ+ people. The right to queer life is not a right that exists in international human-rights law. There is a right to life, and there is a right to live a life free from discrimination, but the idea that we might have a right to live our authentic queer lives is still something that remains to be very much fought for.

Under international human-rights law, there are international conventions and treaties dedicated to the rights of women, racial non-discrimination, disability rights, children's rights, freedom from torture, but there is no dedicated treaty or convention that is binding on states with respect to LGBTQ+ rights. Why? LGBTQ+ rights continue to be controversial at the international level. Many countries refuse to recognise such rights and still impose strict criminal sanctions, including the death penalty. In many countries, LGBTQ+ people are denied basic rights, with minimal protections for those who are fired from their jobs or who want to form and grow a family.

These judgments were just the beginning. In Northern Ireland and the Republic, the prejudices of society have slowly turned to pride. My mother's reaction when I was 15 years old and her journey since to become an ardent supporter of my rights is but one example of this social, cultural, and legal shift. 'You taught me how wrong we all were,' she has told me many times, wishing she could go back to that living room and embrace my young self. When friends would ask her later why I wasn't getting married at home, she would respond patiently that Northern Ireland, to its shame, was yet to enact marriage equality. When I told her that I was trans, she embraced me and said that what mattered was my happiness and my truth. This is how change happens. Not only in our courts, but in our own living rooms and families. It is why I started this story with my own coming-out story. Because simply by living our lives and living our truths, we are battling for a different world, even though it can be hard at times. It gets and will get better.

Chapter 2
Are You Ready for Love?

In my last year at university, the wife of the former first minister of Northern Ireland Peter Robinson, Iris Robinson, also a DUP politician, went on national radio and said that homosexuality was an abomination. 'What I did say was, homosexuality, like all sin, is an abomination,' she clarified some days later to the press. Robinson also stated that we could be 'cured' of our homosexuality. Listening to the segment and the debates following it, I was incensed. Why were the DUP still talking about homosexuality as a sin in 2008 — hadn't we moved on from the campaigns to 'Save Ulster from Sodomy'?

I was deeply in love with a woman I'd met on an Erasmus Programme student exchange and was pining for her — why did my girlfriend live so far away? She was in Barcelona, which was full of an urban queer nightlife. She found the Northern Irish situation and its attitude to queer people extremely difficult to understand. It's like you're stuck in the 1940s, she said, when she came to visit. I tried to tell her it wasn't that bad. But clearly we also had a long way to go.

After graduating from law school, I decided to leave Ireland to pursue my career as a barrister. The island could not be my home anymore; I felt too queer to listen to the bullshit on abomination. I wanted to live my life openly; I wanted to learn to be queer and to find a community. So I followed the footsteps of many other Irish people, and I moved from Dublin to London. London was a different story altogether from the Irish capital. Quickly I made a crew of friends. I went out to gay bars that no longer exist: the Black Cap, the Joiners Arms, Ghetto (when it was in Soho and then on Old Street). I walked into a nightclub in a sweaty basement in East London to find that the woman running it had been my badminton partner at school and we had never come out to each other. In those queer clubs, we found each other and built our communities.

At 22 years old, I still had many life lessons to learn. One of them was that I should stop falling for 'straight' women. My friends kept telling me that it was futile, or that I was not a Jehovah's Witness in the business of conversion (*leading the mildly homosexual into a way of life from which he may never recover*), but I found myself attracted again and again to women who said that they were straight. There was one girl from Dublin who had also moved to London who I desperately fancied. Orla was beautiful with long dark hair, smart, and had been one of the coolest girls at university. She had a hot boyfriend and was friends with fashion designers and the Dublin jet set. She had been a few years above me at

Trinity, but she invited me to her parties. I still don't know why. She would flirt with me all night, dancing in a gold sequin dress to MIA and MGMT, sit on my knee, and then leave with a beautiful boy in a leather trench coat or with a DJ. I would always be crestfallen. My friends would roll their eyes and tell me that I was stupid as it happened again and again.

One evening, I had a small party in my flat. I decided that it would be the night where I would tell her how I felt. I had written a song on my guitar. After a few drinks, we took out the guitar and started singing, as Irish people do. Then I sang her my song, 'The Body Electric'. Here's the first verse:

> Did you miss all those classes on Walt Whitman, when he sang the body electric?
> Have you not heard of Anohni or danced to 'Peaches'
> — are you so heterocentric?
> Can't you see that convention is holding you back from all the pleasures of seduction?
> Loving her or him doesn't really matter, it's all a social construction.

Needless to say, the song did not work. In fact, she left my house early that night to go to a hipster warehouse party in Hackney and got together with leather trench-coat man again. I didn't get the girl, not that night or the years that followed, but I got a song out of it, inspired by Walt Whitman's poem 'I Sing the Body Electric', which is an ode to queerness. *To be surrounded by beautiful, curious, breathing, laughing flesh is enough*'. That's how I felt when I first fell in love with a woman, and I still think that it is a beautiful description of love. More recently, I have come to think of the poem in relation to constitutional litigation on decriminalising homosexuality.

In Ireland, I had learnt in law school that the law is not 'struck in the permafrost' of when the constitution was first drafted; instead, its interpretation evolves. It is a living instrument, and judges breathe life into its meaning. This concept of the living, breathing constitution, an affective constitution, exists in different courts around the world. It has taken on particular importance in constitutional and human-rights cases fighting to decriminalise homosexuality of men and women. *Dudgeon v United Kingdom*, *Norris v Ireland*, and the first United Nations case, *Toonen v Australia*, decided in 1994, were all about privacy rights, but courts were soon hearing arguments that criminalising queer people was wrong — and that such laws violate a whole range of our rights — including our right to love.

My song for Orla ended with the lines, *'It's just two bodies together, don't let them tell you lies. It's just two bodies together, don't let them criminalise.'* At the party, some people laughed at this terrible rhyming scheme, but I felt and still feel the message is important. My song mixed a desire for love, for loving, with a political message. It was heartfelt. It was hopeful and it was real.

We have to decriminalise and repeal laws that criminalise LGBTQ+ lives. We have to denounce the way these laws contribute to the violence and discrimination that queer people face in our day-to-day lives. Decriminalising queerness isn't just about our right to have sex with consenting adults; it's about our right to love and move openly in the world. To be able to love the sparkles and the bangles and to prance out of the closets that they try and legally hide us in.

In London, I fulfilled my dream of becoming a human-rights lawyer. I joined an Inn of Court, had to dine 12 times wearing a gown as part of the strange ritual of becoming a barrister, and joined Doughty Street Chambers, known for its human-rights work. I wanted to work with the law because I believed it could be a vehicle for change, but also because I wanted to tackle how it can be a handmaid of state oppression. This is something that women and queer people know instinctively. We have had to battle discriminatory laws in order to simply get on with our lives. The law that is meant to protect us sometimes screws us over. I wanted to change that, by working on cases that would expand our human-rights protections. I spent the next years working on cases affecting gender-based violence against women, reproductive rights, gender equality, and LGBTQ+ rights.

Ten years after graduating from university, 14 years after first waving books around with rage in the law library, I would get a chance to take on the prejudice I had seen in the *Norris v Attorney General* judgment and do so with pride, as an out queer person. I was ready to argue that our love is beautiful and just as worthy of protection and encouragement from the law. In 2018, it was time to move international human-rights law past its concern about the police entering gay men's bedrooms and to get the United Nations to acknowledge how criminalisation impacts a much broader spectrum of our rights, including women's rights. It was time to show how criminalising homosexuality affects our right to live, love, and be the architects of our own lives.

It was time for Rosanna Flamer-Caldera to take on her government and to win.

As a leading LGBTQ+ activist in Sri Lanka for 25 years, Rosanna had suffered harassment, state persecution, and pressure due to the criminal laws in her country. Back in 1999, she jointly started a queer women's group and worked as a coordinator and activist fighting for queer women's rights. Then in 2004, she formed EQUAL GROUND, as she felt that there was 'more emphasis on gay men's rights in Sri Lanka than for all the queer folks in this country'. EQUAL GROUND was the first mixed LGBTIQ+ organisation in the country, and Rosanna became its executive director, making her a prominent target. By the time I met her, she had had enough. She wanted to shine a spotlight on the intersectional struggle for equality and challenge Sri Lanka's laws that criminalise homosexuality.

As in Ireland, these laws are a colonial legacy. The model law was Section 377 of the *Indian Penal Code 1860*, which punished 'carnal intercourse against the order of nature with any man, woman or animal' and which carried a life sentence. Sri Lanka inherited these colonial laws, which criminalised sex between men. But in the early 1990s, a law-reform proposal was brought to 'equalise' the situation with arguments that the law was 'gender biased' because only gay men were criminalised — so the government decided that it was time to criminalise lesbians too. Section 365A of the *Penal Code 1883* was amended to include sexual conduct between women, replacing the word 'male person' with 'person'. Somehow, 'equality' between the sexes had been used to justify the extension of discrimination, showing just how the law can be manipulated to nefarious ends. The criminal punishment under these laws is up to two years of imprisonment for sexual relations between consenting adults.

Rosanna began to work with the London-based organisation Human Dignity Trust to build her case. But she had a problem. In Sri Lanka, there is no way to challenge criminal laws that have been passed by parliament on the basis that they violate human rights or fundamental constitutional rights. Since Rosanna had no domestic recourse to justice, Human Dignity Trust instructed me and two other barristers, Professor Christine Chinkin and Karon Monaghan KC, to challenge the laws at the level of the United Nations. This was far from straightforward. It had been 30 years since the UN treaty bodies had decided a case on the criminalisation of homosexuality. In 1994, the Human Rights Committee had found that Australia was in violation of international human-rights law for criminalising homosexuality in the state of Tasmania, but there had been no case since that time, when Nicholas Toonen had invoked the right to privacy. There had also been no cases on the criminalisation of women's sexuality.

When I met Rosanna in chambers with a team of

lawyers, she explained that she'd had a hard time coming to terms with her sexuality. With her confidence and charm, and a brightly patterned T-shirt screaming 'queer', it seemed hard to believe. But Rosanna explained that she had come a long way. Her teenage years in Sri Lanka were very difficult due to the discrimination and stigma associated with being a lesbian. Despite our very different upbringings, I immediately identified with this. Having to self-censor our desires and gender expression; having to cover up and diminish who we are; being pushed by society into a closet. Because we certainly aren't born in a closet, but we soon learn to protect ourselves in one.

In that first meeting, Rosanna told us how she had known from a young age that she was different to the other girls in her neighbourhood: how she wasn't feminine and how she hated to wear the dresses that her mother put her in. She was a tomboy who wanted to play games with the boys, wear shorts, and have cropped hair. I really identified with that: I had also played football and wanted desperately to be one of the boys. Rosanna was eight years old when she first realised that she had a crush on another girl. She knew that she had to keep this a secret, like so many of us do. We don't know why; we just know we are transgressing.

Rosanna explained that throughout her adult life she has lived in a society that has tried to make her conform to 'female' stereotypes. She took jobs that forced her to wear a sari. Ultimately, she quit to start her own foundation. She was writing her own life script. But she faced the consequences for being an out lesbian in a country where lesbians were largely invisible. She suffered high-profile attacks in the media, and the police made claims that her LGBTIQ+ advocacy was 'spreading' homosexuality and paedophilia. Rosanna would get harassed on the street because of her 'masculine' attire and her short hair. Obviously she could not complain to the police about the harassment, since she was scared that she would be arrested due to her sexuality. Rosanna feared for her life and the security of her staff at the LGBTQ+ NGO she had founded. She feared that she could be disappeared and never seen again.

The criminal laws not only impacted Rosanna's professional life, but also took a huge toll on her personal life. She found it hard to find a girlfriend in Sri Lanka. She lived in constant anxiety that she would be arrested when she was at home with her girlfriend. In a country where women are expected to become 'good wives' and have children, Rosanna was living a life that flew in the face of compulsory heterosexuality.

Rosanna's situation illustrates how criminalising sexuality is not only about the sex acts, but involves the 'liberty of the person both in its spatial and more transcendent dimensions'. That is how the US Supreme Court put it in 2003 when it held that the criminalisation of homosexuality in Texas violated the US Constitution. Let's have a glance back at that case.

Until the early 2000s, people like me in numerous US states continued to fear criminalisation and arrest for engaging in intimacy, even in their own beds and homes. They feared being humiliated in public through the publication in newspapers about the circumstances of their arrest. They feared obtaining a criminal record. Sometimes, contact with the law would be the way in which people would be outed to their families, friends, and society, resulting in the loss of their jobs. Challenging criminalisation and ensuring that the states no longer sanctioned discrimination against the LGBTQ+ community was a major goal of activists across the US in the wake of the devastation of the HIV crisis.

My American friend who I showed around Dublin grew up in Texas. She left home in 2003 and went to California, where being gay was not a crime. When she was a queer teenager in Austin, it was a criminal offence to engage in same-sex intimacy, for both men and women. She grew up scared of being caught and criminalised. It is even more striking that her father was 60 when the law finally changed and homosexuality was decriminalised in the US. He lived most of his life with the law telling him that his daughter's sexuality was wrong.

All this changed due to the case of *Lawrence v Texas*. Texas is a big red state the size of Europe. With its expanse of sky and desert, two-stepping country music, tornados, and cowboys, it has a population of over 30 million. Until 2003, the state still criminalised 'deviate sexual intercourse'. In 2003, I was in my last year at school. Christina Aguilera had released her single 'Beautiful', which features two men kissing with tongues. *Queer Eye for the Straight Guy* debuted that year, and *Will and Grace* was in its sixth season.

But the case challenging the criminalisation of homosexuality started with the events and arrests that took place in 1998, in a flat in Houston, the biggest city in Texas. One night, two adult men, John Geddes Lawrence and Tyron Garner, were arrested in a second-floor apartment by officers of the Harris County Police Department. Lawrence and Garner were not lovers, but they were drinking in the apartment with Garner's boyfriend, Robert Eubanks. You wouldn't know it from the Supreme Court judgment, but it was Eubanks who called the police on a September night to say that a man (in fact his boyfriend) was going crazy with a gun in an apartment. A complete lie. According to reports, when Lawrence and Garner started to flirt, Eubanks fell into 'a jealous rage', left the apartment, and called the police on them as an act of revenge.

The officers entered the home, to find there was no gun. What the officers exactly saw in that apartment is contested. But the outcome was that the two men were arrested for the offence of sodomy. Lawrence and Garner were handcuffed, held in custody overnight, charged, and convicted. They were ordered to pay a fine and court costs. The criminal complaint described their crime as 'deviate sexual intercourse, namely anal sex, with a member of the same sex (man)'. Imagine having that on your criminal record. Also imagine how scared those two men must have been.

At the time, 13 states criminalised sodomy, but the laws were not generally enforced. That had been the position in Texas up until the early 1990s. Yet the experience of Lawrence and Garner shows how laws that sit on the books can always be used.

Just like Jeffrey Dudgeon in Northern Ireland and David Norris in Ireland, John Geddes Lawrence and Tyron

Garner took their case to courts to overturn their convictions and to make the lives of gay men better in the United States. The men first challenged the sodomy laws in the Texan judicial system. In his book *Flagrant Conduct*, law professor Dale Carpenter recounts how the men and the defence team had to walk to the courtroom through the media and protestors holding up anti-gay signs stating 'God Hates Fags'. They lost their case in the state courts, with the highest court refusing to hear the case, and they wound up in the US Supreme Court.

It took five years to be heard in the Supreme Court, with the case commencing on 26 March 2003. The decision was published in June 2003. This is very recent history. The song of the summer when the court's decision came out was 'Crazy in Love' by Beyoncé and Jay-Z. I listened to that song on CD in our common room in my last year of high school.

The majority opinion was penned by Justice Anthony Kennedy. He starts his judgment off by saying that the case involves 'liberty of the person both in its spatial and more transcendent dimensions'. The Supreme Court recognises that sexual intimacy is just 'one element in a personal bond that is more enduring' and concludes that 'The liberty protected by the Constitution allows homosexual persons the right to make this choice.'

The Supreme Court majority points to the case of *Dudgeon* to counter its previous precedent in *Bowers v Hardwick*. *Bowers* was a 1986 case in which the Supreme Court upheld the constitutionality of the sodomy-law provisions in Georgia. But that was 1986 and now we were in 2003 and courts like the European Court of Human Rights and the UN Human Rights Committee had decided that criminalising homosexuality was incompatible with fundamental human rights. 'Other nations, too, have taken action', Justice Kennedy says.

The United States Supreme Court decision in *Lawrence v Texas* signals an important shift in the development of queer jurisprudence over the course of my youth. Although the discussion also centres on privacy rights, the reasoning goes much further than the European Court of Human Rights in its recognition of the many ways in which criminalisation impacts gay men's lives. The judgment explains that decriminalising same-sex conduct is about liberty and freedom. It's about allowing ourselves to live our authentic lives. 'At the heart of liberty is the right to define one's own concept of existence, of meaning, of the universe, and of the mystery of human life.' Justice Kennedy writes that gay people may seek autonomy just as heterosexual persons do when it comes to consenting private acts of intimacy. We have a right to make our most intimate and personal choices: who we love, go to bed with, and wake up next to. We have a fundamental right to make choices about sexual intimacy.

The Supreme Court majority also recognises that criminal laws, even when they are not enforced, create stigma and have important collateral impacts on the lives of that person. The court explains in one of its most well-known passages that 'When homosexual conduct is made criminal by the law of the State, that declaration in and of itself is an invitation to subject homosexual persons to discrimination both in the public and in the private spheres.'

The court explains that the criminal conviction in Texas for private, consensual homosexual conduct would result in that person being registered as a sex offender in at least four other US states. Such convictions also result in gay men being disqualified from holding certain professions, including in medicine — and, interestingly, interior design. Often a conviction would result in someone losing their job.

The ongoing consequences of a criminal conviction and its marker on a criminal record is a significant point recognised by the Supreme Court. Criminal laws give police powers to come into your homes, into your bedrooms. Even when criminal laws are not enforced, they legitimise the oppressive social and cultural environment in which queer people navigate their lives. Queer people are made to feel like criminals and are treated as such. It encourages families to disown their children or even report them to the police when they find out about their sexuality. The community is placed under surveillance, and state agents can be used to police behaviour and movement. It has a particular impact on young gay people who should be learning about healthy and respectful relationships, respect, consent, autonomy, and love. Instead, it teaches young gay people to have shame, hounds them into the closet, and allows stigma to proliferate.

Criminalising queers has a profound impact on our mental health. As the High Court in Ireland explains in *Norris*, 'One of the effects of criminal sanctions against homosexual acts is to reinforce the misapprehension and general prejudice of the public and increase the anxiety and guilt feelings of homosexuals leading, on occasions, to depression ...' This is why countries like Ireland and the UK have set up legal schemes to expunge criminal records in relation to historic sodomy offences. They were fundamental injustices meted out to queer people.

As the US Supreme Court observes, later generations can see that 'laws once thought necessary and proper in fact serve only to oppress.' The majority found that the Texas statute violated the Due Process Clause of the US Constitution since it violated the rights of the plaintiffs to their liberty. The state should not 'control their destiny by making their private sexual conduct a crime'. The court held that the men were entitled to respect for their private life.

Lawrence and Garner won their case after half a decade, becoming the cause célèbre of the gay-rights movement in the US. Sadly, Garner would die three years later, aged just 39 years old.

Rosanna Flamer-Caldera left Sri Lanka when she was young to live in California for some time, to escape the harsh context of criminalisation and the stigmatisation that goes with it. She lived in San Francisco and got involved in activism, participating in demonstrations and marches. In 1978, she attended her first pride parade, led by Harvey Milk. Then five months after that famous event, Rosanna attended a candlelight vigil after Milk was assassinated.

Rosanna learnt about different techniques and strategies for activism. After years of fighting for LGBTQ+ rights in the US, she decided to return home and to fight for her rights and the rights of her community in Sri Lanka, but the legal and social context there continued to make it difficult for her to live her life, to have relationships, and to be an activist.

After meeting Rosanna a few times and discussing her legal opinions, we decided to file her case in 2018 before the United Nations CEDAW Committee. CEDAW is the Convention on the Elimination of All Forms of Discrimination Against Women. The committee's most important work has been on the issue of gender-based violence against women. Christine Chinkin and I had been part of an expert group advising the committee on a legal document called General Recommendation No. 35. This is an international human-rights law instrument that provides guidance to states to help them understand their human-rights obligations. It makes it absolutely clear that international law requires states to decriminalise women on the basis of their sexuality.

The standard was clear, but there was no legal case clearly setting this position out or properly linking why criminalisation of same-sex conduct violates a woman's right to live a life free from gender-based violence. We wanted the CEDAW Committee to recognise in Rosanna's case that criminalising same-sex intimacy isn't just about what happens in the bedroom, but also about how it impacts a whole range of human rights, including our right to form relationships and family, to live without discrimination, to participate in activism, to have jobs, to live as we want to live, and to love.

Moreover, the legal challenges that had come before the human-rights courts and constitutional courts in many countries did not recognise the specific impact that criminalising same-sex intimacy between women has on their lives. In many cases, the plaintiffs were men who had been targeted by law enforcement, and the plight of lesbians and queer women were simply not considered by the judges. This is despite the fact, as documented by Human Dignity Trust, that around half of the countries that criminalise same-sex conduct between men also criminalise conduct between women.

Rosanna's whole life and career has been dedicated to making the invisible visible. For 20 years she has been working in Sri Lanka, founding organisations that document the violence and state repression faced by lesbian, bisexual, and queer women in her country. As Rosanna explained to us, queer women in Sri Lanka are criminalised by the homosexuality law, but their criminalisation is amplified by other criminal laws regulating women's sexuality, including laws banning adultery. Social attitudes, patriarchal culture, discriminatory laws, and gendered expectations all converge to deny women their ability to live freely.

In many countries, laws exist to prevent women from making decisions about their living situations, leaving their husbands, or even learning to drive. Sometimes queer women can't rent an apartment without the permission of a man, or they face restrictions on inheritance if they are not married. They are denied the exercise of choice over their own bodies. Their battles on the basis of their sex and sexuality differ from those of men. Their private sphere is much wider. Their battles are gendered and layered.

This is because the law in its foundation is paternalistic and patriarchal. The legal system views women as mothers and wives, with duties in the household and towards her husband. Even the Irish Constitution contains a provision that says the state recognises a woman's 'life within the home' and holds that it will 'endeavour to ensure that mothers shall not be obliged by economic necessity to engage in labour to the neglect of their duties in the home'. This gender stereotyping and discrimination is the basis for the control of women's sexuality, which has often been conceived as a form of male property. The view of women as a man's property upon marriage has traditionally and continues to justify legal provisions that hold that women cannot be raped by their husbands. It was only in the 1990s that marital rape was outlawed in the United Kingdom and the Republic of Ireland. In Sri Lanka, where gay sex and lesbian sex are both a crime, marital rape is not a crime. Women continue to be punished in legal systems around the world when men are not for committing adultery or for carrying out sex work. The law is replete with discrimination.

This in turn reinforces societal attitudes. Queer women and trans and non-binary people around the world are persecuted and face a myriad of forms of violence. Anyone who has spent time in a woman's body can speak to this. The fear of walking down the street in the dark. The footsteps behind you. Crossing a road to avoid a group of men. This threat of violence, which is real, is also targeted in specific ways at women who dare to love and show affection to other women, even when such affection is legal. This includes horrendous forms of sexual violence such as rape and coercive marriage practices.

In India, for example, although Section 377 of the *Indian Penal Code* was used by police to target gay men, families would use it to threaten daughters if they did not give up their same-sex relationships. As noted by activist Jaya Sharma, 'While Section 377 is rarely used in court against women, the very presence of such law is used as a mechanism by families to blackmail and threaten their lesbian kin.' In 2018, a court in the state of Kerala ruled that a lesbian couple could live together after one of the women was forcibly detained by her family. The verdict was the first of its kind, and was only decided once the country decriminalised homosexuality.

Our strategy in Rosanna's case was to focus on how criminalisation is a form of discrimination and how it violates women's rights to live a life free from gender-based violence. We argued in our brief to the UN CEDAW Committee that the criminalisation of same-sex activity between women, and the potential for arrest and prosecution, is a form of intersectional discrimination on the grounds of gender and sexual orientation. While the legal provisions criminalising homosexuality in Sri Lanka punish both men and women, Rosanna set out to challenge the criminal amendment to the law specifically punishing women. She argued that by virtue of the intersecting forms of discrimination she faces as a women and a lesbian, the law compounds the discrimination and stigmatisation that lesbian and bisexual women face, making them vulnerable to harassment, vilification, threats, and violence that men don't face or face in a different way.

We also argued that the criminalisation of same-sex activity impacts Rosanna's rights to access justice, since she is unable to get protection or complain to the police to report harassment and violence. Lesbian, gay, bisexual, trans, and intersex persons underreport serious crimes, including rape and violations of bodily autonomy, we explained, because the police will not properly investigate or prosecute these offences — instead, the LGBTQ+ community fear arrest. We argued that this in turn exacerbates gender-based violence against women, including at the hands of community and family. That it creates a context in which lesbians and bisexual women are forced into heterosexual marriages and suffer violations of their right to sexual and bodily autonomy. We also argued that criminalising same-sex conduct between women forms part of entrenched patriarchy as it fixes gender roles, reduces women to reproductive functions, and punishes women who fail to conform with gender stereotypes.

Our arguments also highlighted how Rosanna, given her public profile as an LGBTQ+ advocate and human-rights defender, is particularly vulnerable to discrimination, vilification, surveillance, and harassment. An amicus brief by Professor Dianne Otto, one of the world's leading academics on queer rights, argued that Rosanna's right to public participation has been breached due to these criminal laws and the security protocols that she has to put in place to keep herself, her colleagues, and her family safe. Otto's brief made the significant point that criminalising homosexuality violates our right to be civil-society activists and participants. It impinges on our democratic freedoms.

Finally, we argued that criminalising lesbians and queer women violates the right to family life under international law. The Convention on the Elimination of All Forms of Discrimination Against Women provides that signatory states have an obligation to eliminate discrimination against women in all matters relating to marriage and family relations, and that women should be able to freely decide the number and spacing of their children. We argued that the spirit of this convention is to guarantee and protect women's rights to autonomy and choice, including sexual autonomy and self-determination. We argued that criminalising same-sex intimacy brings consensual private activity into the public domain, allows the police to enter homes and make arrests, and makes it more difficult for someone like Rosanna to find a partner.

We filed on the 23 August 2018. On 6 September, our case was given a major boost when the Indian Supreme Court handed down its decision in *Navtej Singh Johar v Union of India*. In that decision, the court struck down Section 377 and recognised the suffering caused to those who had been criminalised. I read the decision with absolute joy. The Supreme Court's judgment was beautiful and would help contextualise our case in a growing movement towards decriminalisation around the world. The legal provision it struck down was almost identical to the one we were challenging at the UN.

'Denial of self-expression is inviting death ... One defines oneself. That is the glorious form of individuality.' So begins the Supreme Court of India's judgment. The court explains that identity is a form of 'authoring one's own life script where freedom broadens every day'. The court understands the importance for LGBTQ+ individuals of living our authentic queer lives, free from prejudice, rigid and gendered stereotypes, and dogmatic social norms. The Constitution of India, the court explains, protects the right to self-determination, to make a pattern of our own lives, and to express ourselves. It is part of our right to human dignity, and queer people are entitled to it.

Explaining the impact of the criminalisation on our bodies, the Supreme Court states in poetic language: 'The immobility due to fear corrodes the desire to express one's own sexual orientation as a consequence of which the body with flesh and bones feels itself caged and a sense of fear gradually converts itself into a skeleton sans spirit.'

Justice D.Y. Chandrachud explains that the colonial legislation made it criminal for 'consenting adults of the same gender ... to find fulfilment in love'. We have the right to live a life without that fear, to express ourselves, to choose our partners. To love. To write our own life scripts. The judgment sets out beautifully how the Constitution is 'an organic and breathing document with senses which are very much alive to its surroundings', just like the people it sets out to protect. The Constitution has a soul. A consciousness. It has a beating pulse. The Constitution is a body. The Constitution is not composed of dead letters. It is transformative, evolving. The Indian Supreme Court understands the words of Walt Whitman that *to be surrounded by beautiful, curious, breathing, laughing flesh is enough*. We have a right to live and to love.

Striking down Section 377 in India, the court finds that the criminalisation of homosexuality, and associated sex acts, not only impacts gay men but also leads to the surveillance and policing of trans persons or hijras; the court finds that Section 377 'was used as an instrument of harassment and physical abuse against hijras and transgender persons'. The approach of the Indian Supreme Court recalls the way that the US Supreme Court overturned the criminalisation of homosexuality in the United States, in a decision that makes explicit how penalties do much more than prohibit a particular sex act.

This is what we wanted to show the UN too.

On 23 March 2022, four years after we filed Rosanna's case, an email pinged across my screen. The UN CEDAW Committee had found that Sri Lanka was violating Rosanna's fundamental human rights. The judgment states that 'decriminalization of consensual same-sex relations is essential to prevent and protect against violence, discrimination and harmful gender stereotypes'.

The CEDAW Committee made a number of recommendations to Sri Lanka, including a recommendation to decriminalise consensual same-sex conduct between women who have passed the age of consent — to repeal Section 365A of the *Penal Code*. It also made it clear that Sri Lanka should ensure that Rosanna and her organisation can safely and freely carry out their activism and that all victims of gender-based violence, including lesbian, bisexual, trans, and intersex women have access to counselling, health services, and financial support.

In 2024, Rosanna was named by *Time* magazine as one of the 100 most influential people in the world for her advocacy for LGBTQ+ rights and for queer women. But Rosanna is just one of the thousands of activists around the world who are working to challenge the criminalisation of LGBTQ+ people. In 2022, the High Court of Antigua and Barbuda struck down laws that criminalise LGBTQ+ people. Both men and women were criminalised for same-sex sexual intimacy there. This followed court decisions in Belize, Guyana, and Trinidad and Tobago, and was followed by a similar decision in St Kitts and Nevis. In 2023, the Supreme Court of Mauritius issued a decision decriminalising homosexuality on the basis the crime was a colonial law, and in 2024, Friedel Dausab, a gay man from Namibia won a constitutional challenge against sodomy laws in the High Court of Namibia.

According to the Human Dignity Trust, 69 jurisdictions currently criminalise private, consensual same-sex activity. Forty-two countries have specific laws on lesbianism, and in 11 countries the penalty for engaging in private, consensual same-sex activity is the death penalty. Some countries also allow corporal punishment, such as Indonesia, which provides for a punishment of 100 lashes. In April 2024, the Ugandan Constitutional Court rubber-stamped the *Anti-Homosexuality Act 2023*. This law criminalises same-sex consensual conduct with up to life imprisonment, while the death penalty exists for having sex with a person younger than 18.

There is still a long way to go until all LGBTQ+ people around the world are free to live their lives and love who they wish without facing brutal repression, stigmatisation, and sometimes death. But international human-rights law is clear: states must decriminalise.

A few weeks before I visited the Oscar Wilde museum in Dublin, I was in London for Pride. I wasn't there for the parade itself but to meet up with Rosanna. I couldn't wait to see her. She was filming a documentary, *Queer the Way*, about LGBTQ+ activism and how she had set up EQUAL GROUND. I hadn't seen Rosanna since we filed her case with the UN in 2018.

I walked into the barbershop where she was getting her hair cut before marching in the main parade the next day. There would be over 30,000 participants and 1.5 million visitors. A very different prospect to Colombo Pride, which she had recently organised and which had 100 people in attendance. We embraced, and I told her that she hadn't changed at all. It was true: with her short grey hair and colourful patterned shirt, she looked exactly as I had first met her in chambers, when she told me that she wanted to challenge the penal code in Sri Lanka, all those years ago.

She told me that she is hopeful that the government of Sri Lanka will repeal the discriminatory criminalisation law, but that the political context in her country remains difficult. The fight goes on. While it does, Rosanna and the activists like her who make a difference deserve all the recognition, celebration, and protection we can give them. They are our heroes.

Chapter 3
Express Yourself

My gender is trouble. Not in a way that is distressing, but in a way that is instinctively curious. This curiosity grows with my age.

In my youth, I came out to my friends and family, cut my hair, went to my first pride march, and discovered queer joy. I partied in Paris. Started to kiss girls, stopped wearing skirts and heels. I fell in love. I got my heart broken by a girl from Spain. I fell in love with her again. My Erasmus Programme love was in Barcelona, but the job opportunity was in Madrid, so I took it and figured that it would be easier to see her if we were in the same country. I packed my bags, found a room in an apartment through a friend, and moved in with three gay guys and their three boyfriends in a flat that had a steady stream and rotating cast of beautiful gay men. This was Chueca, June 2009. It was pre-Brexit, meaning that we could just move to other countries in Europe.

I moved in during Pride weekend in Madrid. The song 'Colgando en Tus Manos' was on repeat from the gay bar across the road from our apartment. A couple of doors down, there was a leather bar where bears streamed out in the early hours of the morning. The whole neighbourhood was covered in the rainbow flag for that weekend and, as I would soon find out, throughout the year. Chueca was and still is a gaybourhood. I felt safe and joyous. It was only once I moved to Madrid that I felt able to come fully out of the closet. I was 23.

Although we were all from different places, what my flatmates and I had in common was we had come from small towns to a city, looking for urban freedom. We came in search of other gay, lesbian, and queer people — our community. In our hometowns, we felt like we were alone, the only gay in the village. But in Madrid, at least in our bubble, everybody was gay. In the flat, we hosted Eurovision parties full of musical dancers — at one point, the casts of *Grease*, *Spamalot*, and *Cabaret* were all regulars.

We also hosted weekly screenings of LGBTQ+ documentaries and films from my flatmate Borja's DVD collection. The films depicted stories about the lives of gay men. Classics such as *My Beautiful Laundrette*, *Angels in America*, films by Eytan Fox and Gregg Araki. After the films, we stayed up late on the cheap Ikea rental sofas, sharing our own experiences of coming out, homophobia, and queer dreams.

After months of films about the lives and experiences of gay men, which mostly ended with us in tears, I begged the boys for a film about lesbians or queer women, which is how I identified at the time. There was dead silence until Borja, the film convenor, relented. He announced for the next month the film nights would feature lesbians. The room let out an exasperated sigh. One of the boys made a suggestion: what about *Gone in 60 Seconds*? It has cars and Angelina Jolie. Does that count? I rolled my eyes. In the end, over a few weeks, we watched *But I'm a Cheerleader* and *Mulholland Drive*, there was a cinema outing to see *Habitación en Roma*, and the British romcom *Imagine Me and You* got a screening. The boys tolerated the films but largely wanted to see depictions of their own lives on the screen. Or Barbra Streisand.

The films, documentaries, and TV shows we watched over the course of the year in Chueca helped me understand the struggles of our queer community and showed me a version of myself on screen for the first time. You cannot be what you cannot see, as the saying goes. Queer visibility and representation is vital for the LGBTQ+ community. It has been a lifeline for me as I've started my gender journey. I have wanted and needed to read stories written by other trans men about their lives and journeys. I want to find voices to identify with, to guide me, to laugh with and at times despair with. I have wanted to find myself and see myself reflected in the world. I still want to see that trans Hugh Grant getting Julia Roberts in *Notting Hill*. The transness as incidental to the story.

We watched the films because we were desperate for information. To learn more about our lives and those of our queer elders. To learn about what the philosopher Michel Foucault has called 'alternative ways of being'. We wanted to see love, relationships, romance — but mainly we saw death and suffering. What I didn't realise then was just how lucky we were to be able to see these stories on screen. In many countries, it is impossible, a criminal offence, or socially unacceptable to watch or access LGBTQ+ representation. Censorship laws, laws on blasphemy, laws prohibiting the promotion of homosexuality, religious laws, and laws claiming to protect children all converge to silence queer people when we try to speak about our life.

Even as I write this book, I wonder, how many countries would it be banned in today? Would it even be banned in some states in the US? In too many countries, authors, artists, creatives, and advocates are silenced through arrest and censorship. This is why we must fight for free speech as a queer-rights issue.

———

A few months ago, I went to my American friend's house, where she hosts a regular poetry night. I had printed out two poems to read. 'Two Loves' by Lord Alfred Douglas, the poet with whom Oscar Wilde was tragically enamoured, and the 'The Love That Dares to Speak Its Name' by James Kirkup, which caused a furor when it was printed in the *Gay News* in 1976. The title of the poem echoes the last line of 'Two Loves':

> Then sighing, said the other, 'Have thy will,
> I am the love that dare not speak its name.'

The poems were not in keeping with what I usually read aloud on the poetry nights (Frank O'Hara, Ocean Vuong, Safia Elhillo, if you're curious). I ended my reading with an explanation. In 1976, an individual conservative zealot called Mary Whitehouse brought a private prosecution against *Gay News* and the newspaper's editor for publishing Kirkup's poem. In England, anyone can bring a private prosecution for a criminal offence, which is very problematic since it can be weaponised by the powerful against queers or women. Whitehouse decided to prosecute the paper and the editor, Denis Lemon, for the crime of blasphemy.

Blasphemy was made a crime with the aim of punishing those who reproach the Christian religion — or to be more exact, the Church of England. In a case called *Gathercole's Case*, from 1838, the courts established that a person could attack Judaism, Islam, or any sect of the Christian religion 'save the established religion of the country'. That the laws on blasphemy did not extend to other religions was affirmed once again in 1991 following the publication of *The Satanic Verses* by Salman Rushdie. Blasphemy was a criminal offence in England and Wales until 2008. It is still a criminal offence in Northern Ireland. At the time of the *Gay News* prosecution in the 1970s, it was seldom invoked, but it was still on the books and could be prosecuted with an unlimited penalty.

Denis Lemon and his newspaper ended up in court. *Gay News* was represented by an up-and-coming Australian lawyer, now Geoffrey Robertson KC, who I am proud to count as a colleague. He has recounted how Whitehouse held prayer meetings in the corridors outside the courtroom, and how the judge explained to the jury that his own summing up speech had been inspired by God. In the broader context of social homophobia at the time, it is not a huge surprise that in 1977 the jury found Lemon and *Gay News* guilty. Lemon was the last person in England to be found guilty by a jury for blasphemy. He was fined and sentenced to nine months in jail, suspended. This was later quashed on appeal.

A hush fell over the room when I explained why I had read the poems. How the first poem had been used against Oscar Wilde in his trial, and how the second poem had led to the criminal conviction of a newspaper editor. It was not all bad news, I reassured the artists gathered in the room as I saw the legal gloom settle above their heads. The circulation of *Gay News* rose with publicity from the trial, and Christian crusaders in the UK may no longer take it upon themselves to silence queer speech through accusations of blasphemy.

But in countries around the world, similar laws are being used to ban queer people from speaking. In 2017 in Ireland, after gay marriage had come in, the police force received a complaint and were asked to investigate the author Stephen Fry for blasphemy after he described God as 'capricious', 'mean minded', and 'stupid' for allowing so much suffering in the world. No criminal charges were brought, and in 2018 Ireland abolished the crime of blasphemy through a referendum. In Kenya, which still criminalises homosexuality, the laws on blasphemy and obscenity have both been cited as grounds for banning award-winning documentaries and films such as *Rafiki* and *I Am Samuel*.

Censorship of LGBTQ+ representation has also been

achieved through the criminal offence of obscenity. This has long been used to censor and seize depictions of queer desire, including those between women. In the UK, the *Obscene Publications Act 1857* elevated the common-law offence of engendering 'revulsion, disgust or outrage' into a statutory crime. It sought to uphold public morals, with one judge explaining that the test was what a father could read aloud in his own home.

In 1928, a magistrates' court in England ordered that the now cult lesbian classic *The Well of Loneliness* be destroyed after finding that the book by Radclyffe Hall constituted obscene libel. The judge, Sir Chartres Biron, found that although lesbianism was not a crime, the love and relationships in the books would be criminal offences if the story had been about men and would therefore involve 'the most horrible, unnnatural and disgusting obscenity'. The judge ordered that the book be banned, since 'Everybody, all the characters in the book, who indulge in these vices are presented to be attractive people, and put forward for our admiration, and those who object to these vices are sneered at in the book as prejudiced, foolish and cruel'. The person who had led the crusade against the book, newspaper editor James Douglas, wrote in *The Sunday Express*, 'I would rather give a healthy boy or healthy girl a phial of prussic acid than this novel', which is a pretty extreme thing to say. He would rather administer cyanide to children than let them read about lesbians. It would take another 20 years before the book was published again in England.

British obscenity laws continued to be enforced well

into the 1980s and in fact still exist. On 10 April 1984, Her Majesty's Customs and Excise office raided Gay's the Word, a bookshop in Marchmont Street, Bloomsbury.

Today, the pedestrian crossings at the top of the street have been painted in the colours of the trans flag, and the small shop is filled to the brim with books by queer authors and about queer lives. I stop by every time I'm in London and ask the booksellers to recommend me books. Recently, I've been walking out with armfuls of books by Thomas Page McBee, Emerson Whitney, Paul Preciado, and Kaya Wilson.

It enrages me that back in April 1984, when my parents were dating in London, officers raided the bookshop and the homes of two of its staff, impounding books in what was called 'Operation Tiger'. The officers seized books by Tennessee Williams, Gore Vidal, and Christopher Isherwood on the basis that the material was indecent and obscene and the books 'had the name of a homosexual author on the cover'. The officers also seized feminist books, including *Feminism in the '80s: facing down the right* by Charlotte Bunch. I couldn't believe it when I searched through the list of seized books. I used to teach Bunch's writing in a women's human-rights course and had no idea she'd been censored. The books were being imported from stores in the US, including Giovanni's Room, a famous gay bookstore in Philadelphia, as much of the literature at that time was being written and published in the US.

These bookstores not only provided queer people with access to books about our lives in an age when there was no internet, but also served as local hubs for LGBTQ+ activism, including HIV activism and the organisation of pride parades and protests. They were and still are community spaces. We must take care of them.

The seizures threatened to destroy their business. Gay's the Word challenged the government's actions, and in return HM Customs and Excise brought 100 criminal charges against nine staff members of the shop. The bookshop called up a young Geoffrey Robertson to represent them.

The charges were eventually dropped. Not because a judge or jury acquitted the booksellers, but because by a stroke of good luck the European Court of Justice in Luxembourg handed down judgment in a case involving the importation of sex dolls into the UK. If British obscenity laws didn't prohibit the marketing and selling of domestic sex dolls, the same laws could hardly be used for seizing and banning books like *Cat on a Hot Tin Roof* and *Meat: how men look, act, walk, talk, dress, undress, taste & smell*.

Recently, Geoffrey told me that he went to the bookshop to celebrate the 40th anniversary of this victory. There are cases we continue to celebrate for decades afterwards.

Today, it isn't just blasphemy and obscenity laws that are used to silence queer expression; it is the more nebulous and insidious concept of 'promoting homosexuality', which is relied upon to censor, to ban books, and to arrest activists for doing something as simple as waving a rainbow flag. Governments around the world have enacted or are passing a number of laws that criminalise or sanction the promotion of homosexuality, otherwise known as 'gay propaganda laws'. Countries such as Hungary, Lithuania, and Russia have all enacted laws that claim to protect children but in fact punish queer people for advocating for LGBTQ+ rights. Many of these laws prevent discussion of queer rights or issues to schoolchildren. Some extend far beyond that to criminalise activism on this issue more generally.

An early version of a gay propaganda law existed in England and Wales until 2003: Section 28 of the *Local Government Act 1988*. This banned the promotion of homosexuality or the promotion of 'teaching in any maintained school of the acceptability of homosexuality as a pretended family relationship'. The political debates at the time show the virulent homophobic attitudes of politicians and counsellors. The leader of Staffordshire County Council is reported as stating that 'As a cure I would put 90 per cent of queers in the ruddy gas chamber.' The impact of Section 28 has been well documented. Paul Baker explains in his book *Outrageous!* that 'Instead of children being taught the inalienable right to be gay, Section 28 implicitly taught everyone to be homophobic'. Books were removed from libraries, teachers practised self-censorship and did not come out at school in case they were fired, and young gays were brought up in an environment that tolerated their bullying and silenced any representation or learning about their lives.

My American friend, a passionate book lover, has told me of the similar law put in place in her home state of Texas in 2023. The law bans books that are 'sexually explicit, pervasively vulgar or educationally unsuitable in public schools', resulting in the removal of books that feature LGBTQ+ themes and characters from schools across the state. This has led to teachers losing their jobs or resigning. The former Republican state politician for Texas Matt Kraus published a list of 850 books he would like to see banned from schools. When I looked down the list, I saw that most of them were about feminism, critical race theory, reproductive rights, and stories about being queer. Ocean Vuong posted on social media that his book *On Earth We're Briefly Gorgeous* had been banned. This book isn't on Kraus's list, but it would certainly fit. In response to the law, queer teenagers in Texas and elsewhere are fighting back by creating their own clandestine libraries of the banned books, their curiosity aroused by the book banning.

Texas is currently on top of the leader board of US states banning books. But the laws in Texas are mirrored in many other states. In March 2022, Florida governor Ron DeSantis signed into law the *Parental Rights in Education Act*. Florida is the same state in which a gunman killed 49 people at Pulse, a gay nightclub in Orlando, in 2016. The new law, colloquially referred to as *Don't Say Gay*, bans teachers from holding discussions about sexual orientation or gender identity in public schools with kids up to age eight, while discussions must be 'age appropriate' for older children. In 2023, it was reported that a Florida school district ordered the removal of all books with gay characters, before an outcry prevented this.

DeSantis's press secretary suggested that those opposing the Act are grooming children. Following another mass shooting, at Club Q in Colorado in November 2022, many journalists and activists have drawn attention to growing and hateful rhetoric in the US. Arwa Mahdawi writing in *The Guardian* commented that the massacre felt 'inevitable'. She explains:

> Over the past year there has been an escalation in dangerously dehumanising anti-LGBTQ+ rhetoric. The idea that LGBTQ+ people are 'groomers' and paedophiles has become a mainstream conservative talking point pushed by everyone from Fox News to Republican politicians.

She pointed to the press secretary in Florida as an example of how queer people are increasingly being referred to as 'groomers' and 'paedophiles' and with it has come an increase in violence, which includes bomb threats and killings.

Don't Say Gay has been challenged, with high-profile lawyer Roberta Kaplan representing those seeking to overturn the book bans. In March 2024, the case was settled. The settlement clarified that students and teachers can talk about LGBTQ+ issues as long as their discussions don't form part of the formal curriculum. The settlement also states that books cannot be banned from libraries just for having queer content in them, if they aren't part of the formal classroom instruction. Governor DeSantis's office responded that the law remains in force and that it will 'keep radical gender and sexual ideology out of the classrooms of public school children'.

Roberta explained to me over a call that *Don't Say Gay* is a broader part of the chipping away of rights in the US, that gays and lesbians are being denied services, and that families with trans children in states such as Texas are moving away due to bans on gender-affirming care for young people. Book bans are now at their highest level ever recorded in the US. PEN America estimates that over 10,000 books were banned in public schools in 2023–2024, with the bans overwhelmingly targeting books about queer people and people of colour. It's hard to understand how, in a country with such strong free-speech protections, the book bans can pass constitutional muster. Free speech is a fundamental human right and a cornerstone of democratic society — American society in particular. International and regional human-rights courts have explained that free speech and expression also includes our right to express our gender expression. It is fundamentally important to the way we define ourselves and tell stories about our own lives, a basic condition for an individual's self-fulfilment. Importantly, the right also includes the right to receive information, including a public interest in being able to listen to people's life stories and experiences. There is no place for censoring queer life scripts.

Gay propaganda laws fly in the face of free-speech standards and also those that require states to provide children with comprehensive sexuality education to prepare them for safe and fulfilling love lives. The latter standards emphasise that such education should be age-appropriate and ensure that children can make informed choices and protect themselves in the digital age. Yet sexuality education continues to be attacked as 'propaganda in favour of homosexuality', when really it is a human right for children and adolescents to have information that equips them to understand their own sexuality.

In March 2023, the Office of the United Nations High Commissioner for Human Rights published a guide making it clear that comprehensive sexuality education should promote gender equality, the empowerment of women and girls, empathy, respect, consent, and diversity, as well as ensuring that it is non-discriminatory. States are called on to guarantee that curricula include sexual and gender diversity as well as dismantling patriarchal gender stereotypes. Today, young people around the world are running their own awareness-raising campaigns due to the lack of comprehensive sexuality education. Chanel Contos, a young Australian feminist, has launched a campaign called Teach Us Consent, highlighting how sexual assault continues to be a pervasive issue for girls in schools.

Meanwhile, the laws that ban the promotion of homosexuality are being used not only to ban books and curtail sex education, but also to suppress activism and legal advocacy. I was shocked to find out that Sibongile Ndashe, an amazing feminist South African lawyer I know, had been arrested in relation to her human-rights work. In 2017, lawyers from the wonderful human-rights organisation ISLA (Initiative for Strategic Litigation in Africa), including Sibongile, were detained in Tanzania under laws for 'promoting homosexuality'. The lawyers had gathered to discuss bringing a case against the Tanzanian government, which had reportedly been shutting down HIV centres and clamping down on LGBTQ+ rights.

After their arrest, Sibongile and two of her colleagues were deported from Tanzania. She challenged the arrest, detention, and deportation, but she could not attend the court hearing, because she was still banned from the country. The court did not provide the ISLA lawyers with interpreters, and they were initially denied legal representation. Following a court hearing, Sibongile lost her case. The court legitimised the arrest and detention on the basis that advocacy on behalf of men who have sex with other men and trans people amounted to a contravention of the law, since 'homosexual practices are contrary to the laws of Tanzania'. When I last spoke to Sibongile, she told me they were still considering how and whether to appeal the decision.

The punishment for defending and advocating for queer rights can be even more extreme. In 2021, the gender-nonconforming human-rights defender Zahra Seddiqi Hamedani was arrested and detained while trying to flee Iran to seek protection in Türkiye. On 5 September 2022, she was sentenced to death for the crime of 'spreading corruption on earth'. At the time of writing, she remains in prison.

These are examples of the curtailment of free speech for queer people. But free speech is not only a shield; it is also a sword used to attack our rights. As queer people have made important strides in securing legal protections such as anti-discrimination and equality laws, employment protections, and gay marriage, a legal backlash can be seen, with a fierce battle being fought over the provision of goods and services. At the heart of these cases, religious service providers are arguing that anti-discrimination laws cannot trump their rights to free speech.

Can a bakery refuse to sell someone a cake iced with the message 'Support Gay Marriage' because the owners of the bakery believe that gay marriage is unacceptable to God? Can a baker refuse to bake a cake if it's a cake for a gay wedding? Can someone who runs a B&B refuse a room to a gay couple? Can a registrar refuse to marry a gay couple? What happens when someone's human right to their religious belief and freedom compete against other human rights, such as the right to non-discrimination and equality? How do the courts find a balance? What role does free speech play in this? These are some of the questions that courts in different countries have asked themselves over the last ten years.

Let's go back once again to Northern Ireland, where we met Jeffrey Dudgeon, only now homosexuality is legal. In 2014, Gareth Lee visited a family-run bakery in Belfast called Ashers Bakery and asked them to bake him a cake with the words 'Support Gay Marriage' along with an image of Bert and Ernie from *Sesame Street*. At the time he made the order and paid £36.50 for the cake, gay marriage was unavailable in Northern Ireland (it did not come in until early 2020). A few days later, Lee got a call to say that he would receive a refund and that the bakery could not provide him with the cake due to the message on it. It was contrary to their Christian beliefs they explained. The proprietor, Amy McArthur, apologised.

The bakery that Lee walked into was run by the McArthur family, who owned six shops in Northern Ireland. The name of the bakery was derived from Genesis 49:20 — 'Bread from

Asher shall be rich, And he shall yield royal dainties' — but Lee did not know this. He also didn't know that the McArthur family holds the following religious beliefs: (a) the only form of full sexual expression consistent with biblical teaching (and therefore acceptable to God) is between a man and a woman within marriage, and (b) the only form of marriage consistent with biblical teaching is that between a man and a woman. He had previously bought cakes there and didn't know anything about the religious views of the owners.

After the refusal of his order, Lee decided to bring a case against the bakery and sought damages of £500. He argued that the refusal to provide him with a cake was discrimination based on his sexual orientation and that the treatment violated equality laws. He initially won, with the courts and Court of Appeal finding that the refusal to provide him with the cake was 'associative direct discrimination' on the grounds of his sexuality. The attorney-general of Northern Ireland decided to appeal the case. It went to the Supreme Court.

On 10 October 2018, the UK Supreme Court handed down its judgment in 'the gay cake case'. The Supreme Court held that 'in a nutshell, the objection was to the message and not to any particular person or persons' and therefore it did not constitute discrimination. A straight person could have equally ordered a cake asking for the same message of support for gay marriage. The bakers were objecting to this statement rather than refusing a service to a gay man. Lady Brenda Hale writing for the majority of the Supreme Court said:

It is deeply humiliating, and an affront to human dignity, to deny someone a service because of that person's race, gender, disability, sexual orientation or any of the other protected personal characteristics. But that is not what happened in this case and it does the project of equal treatment no favours to seek to extend it beyond its proper scope.

The court held that support for gay marriage is not a proxy for someone's sexuality; his treatment was 'to the message, and not the messenger'. The court explained that the case was not comparable to a situation where people are being refused jobs, accommodation, or business because of their sexuality. But rather 'It is more akin to a Christian printing business being required to print leaflets promoting an atheist message.'

The court explained that under human-rights law, different rights must be balanced. In this case, equality laws had to be balanced against freedom of thought, conscience, and religion, and this, along with free speech, is 'one of the foundations of a democratic society'. It is a right that believers and Christians have, but also protects atheists, sceptics, and the unconcerned. It protects the freedom to believe and not to believe. The right under international human-rights law also includes a component of the right to manifest a belief, but this is not an absolute right.

The right to free speech also comes into play because this right protects the freedom not to be obliged to manifest beliefs that you do not hold. The right to freedom of expression includes the right not to express an opinion or belief. The courts have made it clear that 'nobody should be forced to have or express a political opinion in which he does not believe'. In the United States, this has been termed 'compelled speech', with the courts there finding that 'the right to freedom of thought protected by the First Amendment against state action includes both the right to speak freely and the right to refrain from speaking at all'. The UK Supreme Court therefore held that people who supply goods, facilities, and services should not be compelled to express messages with which they disagree when these relate to their deeply held religious and philosophical beliefs.

Gareth Lee lost his case and appealed to the European Court of Human Rights, which dismissed his case as inadmissible. Speaking to the press, he expressed disappointment with the Supreme Court decision: 'None of us should be expected to have to figure out the beliefs of a company's owners before going into their shop or paying for their services.'

The Supreme Court's decision in the gay cake case was different to its earlier decision in *Bull v Hall*, which was decided by a similarly constituted court five years beforehand. In that case, the court was asked to consider whether it was lawful for Christian hotelkeepers to refuse a double bed to a same-sex couple, on the basis that they believed that it was sinful. Steven Preddy and Martin Hall, who were in a civil partnership, booked a hotel in Cornwall to go on a staycation in 2008. The hotel had a clause that double-bed accommodation was only available to married heterosexual couples, and that unmarried couples — gay and straight — were only allowed to stay in rooms with twin beds or in singles. But when he booked his hotel room, Steven Preddy wasn't told about this. It was only when they arrived at the hotel that they were informed of the policy. The gay couple left the hotel, decided to find alternative accommodation, and to take a case against the hotel owners. So had they been discriminated against?

Like many gay people in the UK, I followed this case very closely. When I heard about the case from some of the human-rights lawyers involved in my chambers, I immediately thought of my own experiences. On one of the first holidays I went on with my first girlfriend, Olivia, we travelled to Venice to visit her friends and ex-girlfriend. We'd booked a hotel room with a double bed. When we arrived, the receptionist looked at us and denied the request. I saw Olivia blush as she spoke to him in Venetian, and although I didn't understand the words, I knew what was being said. We were shown a room with two single beds. We accepted the situation with indignation but also with a sense that perhaps what we were doing was shameful. We were young and lacked the empowerment necessary to fight for our rights and the economic means to simply change hotels at the last minute. It was the first time I realised that as queer people we can be denied services and hospitality simply on the basis of our sexuality.

Preddy and Hall took on the fight for all of us, the whole way to the Supreme Court. The first question the court asked itself was whether the refusal to provide a double bed to the couple constituted discrimination. The religious hotel owners argued that they were not discriminating against the couple on the basis of their sexual orientation but on the grounds that they were not married to one another. They would have equally refused a heterosexual unmarried couple, they said. The argument against them was that heterosexual people could marry, while the law did not provide that option to gay couples — meaning that the policy would always discriminate against them.

In the Supreme Court, the lawyer for the religious hotelkeepers tried to argue that gay couples, including those in civil partnerships, were not discriminated against, since gay people were able to marry. They could marry people of the opposite sex. It was simply that they were not free to marry a person who shared their own orientation. The court was not convinced by this argument, although as an aside the majority judgment noted that history abounds with people who have done so: 'I would instance the long, happy and fruitful marriage of Victoria Sackville-West and Harold Nicolson', said Lady Hale. This obscure reference is to the poet Vita Sackville-West, who was a lover of Virginia Woolf and the inspiration for her novel *Orlando*. Vita had relationships with women throughout her marriage with Harold, who also had same-sex relationships. In 1917, before she met Virginia, Vita had eloped with another woman and was brought back to England by her husband. Of course, having same-sex marriages was never open to Vita and Harold. And it is doubtful that Constance Wilde was happy with her situation.

In reaching their conclusion that the gay couple had been discriminated against, the Supreme Court explained that the criterion of marriage or civil partnership was 'indissociable' from someone's sexual orientation since the two institutions were (at that time) mutually exclusive.

Lady Hale explained that 'there is an exact correspondence between the advantage conferred and the disadvantage imposed in allowing a double bed to the one and denying it to the other.' Lady Hale found that the religious hotel owners would have denied not only heterosexual unmarried couples a double bed, but also gay couples married abroad, since their true criteria was a not marriage but a union between a man and a woman. This is something gay couples could never satisfy. The court found that the criterion 'is specific to those of homosexual orientation'. The Supreme Court concluded in this case that the gay couple had been discriminated against by the religious owners.

The owners argued that they should not be compelled to run their business in a way that conflicts with their views of allowing sin to occur under their hotel roof, and that they should not be obliged to allow unmarried couples to share a bed. But the court did not agree. It found that since same-sex couples could now enter a mutual, stable, long-term commitment — an 'equivalent' of marriage — through a civil partnership, then the suppliers of good, facilities, and services should treat them in the same way as a married couple.

> To permit someone to discriminate on the ground that he did not believe that persons of homosexual orientation should be treated equally with persons of heterosexual orientation would be to create a class of people who were exempt from the discrimination legislation. We do not normally allow people to behave in a way which the law prohibits because they disagree with the law. But to allow discrimination against persons of homosexual

orientation (or indeed heterosexual orientation) because of belief, however sincerely held, and however based on the biblical text, would be to do just that.

The court held that the hotelkeepers were free to manifest their religion but that they had to do so in a way that was not discriminatory. They could continue to deny double beds to unmarried couples, including gay couples, so long as they denied them to married couples too. The UK court turned to the jurisprudence of the Constitutional Court of South Africa to emphasise that as people and rights-holders we live in our bodies, our communities, and that expressing our sexuality 'requires a partner, real or imagined'. The court explained that queer people have long been denied the possibility of fulfilling ourselves through relationships, as these were denied to us. Our human dignity was denied by the law. 'But we should not underestimate the continuing legacy of those centuries of discrimination, persecution even, which is still going on in many parts of the world.'

This judgment was celebrated in 2013. Five years later, in the gay cake case, the Supreme Court reached a different conclusion, based on the message on the cake. Are the two scenarios really so different? And what if Ashers had refused to bake a wedding cake for a gay couple with no message on it? What if a baker simply refused to bake a cake on the basis that it was for a gay wedding? Would that be refusal based on a message or refusal based on a class of people?

While the judgment was being prepared in the

Northern Irish gay cake case, the Supreme Court of the United States of America handed down its judgment in the American gay cake case. It was by complete coincidence that in two different countries, the supreme courts were considering cases about gay cake.

In 2012, a gay couple, Charlie Craig and David Mullins, went into Masterpiece Cakeshop, a bakery in Colorado, to order a wedding cake. Same-sex marriage wasn't available yet in their state, but they were planning to have a celebration with their friends and family after marrying in Massachusetts. But when the couple walked into the cake shop with Craig's mother, they were informed that the shop would not make a cake for a same-sex wedding. The owner of the cake shop explained that he was a Christian and that making a wedding cake for a gay couple would be contrary to his core religious beliefs. The couple were stunned, and turned to the Colorado Civil Rights Commission.

Colorado has an anti-discrimination act that prohibits businesses from discriminating against people on different grounds, including on the basis of a person's sexuality. It provides:

> It is discriminatory practice and unlawful for a person, directly or indirectly, to refuse, withhold from, or deny to an individual or a group, because of disability, race, creed, color, sex, sexual orientation, marital status, national origin, or ancestry, the full and equal enjoyment of the goods, services, facilities, privileges, advantages, or accommodations of a place of public accommodation.

The Colorado Civil Rights Commission found that Jack Philips, the Christian baker, had violated Colorado's anti-discrimination law. The case wound its way up through the courts and eventually made its way to the US Supreme Court. By the time they heard the case, Colorado had legalised gay marriage as mandated by the Supreme Court.

On 4 June 2018, the Supreme Court found against the Colorado Civil Rights Commission, but it based its decision on procedural issues and the way that Philips had been treated by the commission rather than the substantive question in the case. The question — as to whether it would violate Philips's rights to religion or free speech to force the cake shop to design and bake a cake for a gay wedding — remained unanswered. The court did make statements that objections to gay marriage 'do not allow business owners and other actors in the economy and in society to deny protected persons equal access to goods and services' and that there would be serious stigma imposed on gay people if businesses who object to gay marriages for moral and religious reasons are 'allowed to put up signs saying "no goods or services will be sold if they will be used for gay marriages"'.

The UK Supreme Court ended up writing a postscript to the US judgment when it handed down its own judgment four months later. Lady Hale wrote:

> The important message from the *Masterpiece Bakery* case is that there is a clear distinction between refusing to produce a cake conveying a particular message, for any customer who wants such a cake, and refusing to

produce a cake for the particular customer who wants it because of that customer's characteristics.

She held that, on the facts of the Northern Irish case, there was no doubt that the bakers would have refused to supply anybody, gay or straight, with a cake with words supporting gay marriage on it, 'So there was no discrimination on grounds of sexual orientation.' The court found this was different to the facts in the US case. But most people commenting on the US case found that the message of that court was far from clear. Professor Steve Vladeck, the CNN Supreme Court analyst, commented that the decision 'leaves for another day virtually all of the major constitutional questions that this case presented'.

The legal uncertainty in the US led to a raft of lower-court decisions concerning refusals. Florists refused to provide flowers for gay weddings; some photographers refused their services to gay engaged couples too. Is this discrimination? Or is it the protection of religious freedom? Or of free speech? Whose speech and whose rights are being protected? Should gay people simply take their business elsewhere? It seems that with the increasing number of refusals, the law was once again failing to act as a shield.

In June 2023, the US Supreme Court, now stacked with conservative judges, was called upon to answer these questions once again. 303 Creative is a web-design company owned and run by a Christian website designer, Lorie Smith. Smith offers website services and she wanted to extend her business to couples seeking websites for their weddings. She would provide the couples with text, artwork, and videos to celebrate and convey their unique love stories. All of the text and artwork would be 'original', 'customised', and 'tailored'. Smith decided to bring a legal case because she was worried that if she entered the wedding-website business, 'the State will force her to convey messages inconsistent with her belief that marriage should be reserved to unions between one man and one woman'. She asserted that Colorado anti-discrimination law was violating her free-speech rights, and that her constitutional rights protect her from being compelled to speak what she does not believe. She was challenging the same anti-discrimination law at issue in the *Masterpiece Cakeshop* case. But this time, instead of a wedding cake, the court had to consider wedding websites.

In her case, Smith stated that she was 'willing to work with all people regardless of classifications such as race, creed, sexual orientation, and gender' but she would not produce content that 'contradicts biblical truth'. She explained that since she creates her artwork, the speech involved is expressive speech. Should the law compel her to produce a website and artwork for a same-sex marriage? Could she refuse to create a website for a gay couple for their wedding? Would doing so violate her free-speech and religious rights?

Reading the facts of the matter, the outcome would seem to be straightforward, since this case is about services. As Lady Hale said in the case of the hotelkeepers, we do not allow people to disobey the law and discriminate because their religious beliefs disagree with the law. Could the fact that Smith disagreed with same-sex marriage, now recognised as a constitutionally protected right in the US, mean that she could deny her services on equal terms?

The majority judgment was delivered by Justice Neil Gorsuch, who was nominated by Donald Trump in 2017. He is a conservative appointee but has taken some progressive positions in previous Supreme Court cases. For example, Justice Gorsuch wrote the majority opinion in a significant 2020 case called *Bostock v Clayton County*. This was in fact three cases that were heard together by the Supreme Court. In those cases, the court was asked to determine whether someone could be fired for being gay or trans. Gerald Bostock had been working with Clayton County for ten years before he began to participate in a gay softball league; he was fired for 'conduct unbecoming of its employees'. Donald Zarda had worked as a skydiving instructor in New York; he mentioned that he was gay and was fired. Aimee Stephens had worked in a funeral home in Michigan; she let her employer know after two years of working for them that she was transitioning, and the funeral home fired her, saying, 'this is not going to work out'.

In the majority judgment, Justice Gorsuch held that an employer who fires an individual employee merely for being gay or trans violates the *Civil Rights Act*. The judgment found that the wording of the law was unambiguous: 'an individual's homosexuality or transgender status is not relevant to employment decisions. That's because it is impossible to discriminate against a person for being homosexual or transgender without discriminating against that individual based on sex.' Three Supreme Court justices disagreed with his assessment: Thomas, Alito, and Kavanaugh, the most conservative judges of the court. But the majority of the court made it clear: you can't fire someone in the US just for being gay or trans.

Justice Gorsuch was also part of the court's majority in denying Kim Davis a chance to have her case heard in the Supreme Court. She was a county clerk in Kentucky who refused to grant a marriage licence to a gay couple on the basis that it would violate her religious beliefs. She lost her case and was ordered to pay the couple $100,000.

But in other cases, he had joined Thomas and Alito, who have expressed the opinion that the Supreme Court's gay-marriage decision in *Obergefell v Hodges* was an affront to religious belief. Most famously, he joined the conversative judges in *Dobbs v Jackson*, overturning *Roe v Wade*.

So how would Gorsuch frame the case of 303 Creative and answer the question the majority decided to address: can a state force someone who provides her own expressive services to abandon her conscience and speak *its* preferred message instead? The outcome of the case was determined by the framing of the question. The court did not ask whether someone could ignore equal law and refuse to provide services based on their own religious beliefs — or, some would say, prejudices.

In the first paragraph of his judgment, the judge explains, 'Colorado does not just seek to ensure the sale of goods or services on equal terms. It seeks to use its law to compel an individual to create speech she does not believe'. The Supreme Court held that the anti-discrimination law in Colorado represented an impermissible abridgment of Smith's free-speech rights, as it compelled her to speak or face sanctions. The judge explained that to hold otherwise would be problematic because the 'principle would allow the government to force all manner of artists, speechwriters, and others whose services involve speech to speak what they do not believe on pain of penalty'. The court used the following examples: the government could require 'an unwilling Muslim movie director to make a film with a Zionist message' or 'an atheist muralist to accept a commission celebrating Evangelical zeal' or 'a gay web designer to create websites for a group advocating against same-sex marriage'. The court held that compelling Lorie Smith to accept commissions to create websites for same-sex marriages would infringe her First Amendment rights. The majority's judgment understands a wedding website as a form of artwork, but is that really the right analogy? Is a website comparable to a film, painting, or mural? Or is it a different type of work, open to the public and online?

Justice Sonia Sotomayor (joined by two other judges) penned a vociferous dissent. She noted that, only five years prior, the court had held in *Masterpiece Cakeshop* that business owners could not discriminate and deny services based on an objection to gay marriage, but now 'the Court, for the first time in its history, grants a business open to the public a constitutional right to refuse to serve members of a protected class'. She wrote that there is a backlash against gender equality and sexual minorities in the United States and that the majority had failed to understand that 'the act of discrimination has never constituted protected expression' under free-speech rights. The Constitution does not protect a right to refuse a service. The dissenting judgment echoes the decision in *Bull v Hall* in the UK, in which Lady Hale held that the hotel owners had to provide double rooms to everybody or nobody. Justice Sotomayor explains:

A public accommodations law does not force anyone to start a business, or to hold out the business's goods or services to the public at large. The law also does not compel any business to sell any particular good or service. But if a business chooses to profit from the public market, which is established and maintained by the state, the state may require the business to abide by a legal norm of nondiscrimination.

As she put it in her judgment: 'LGBT people do not seek any special treatment. All they seek is to exist in public.' We just want to be treated in the same way as everyone else.

Following the decision, *Time* magazine reported that the implications of the judgment were immediately being felt. New cases have been filed to consider whether the creation of wedding cakes constitutes commercial speech in the same way that Lorie Smith's websites do. What about floral arrangements? What about a funeral home that decides to refuse a burial request from a surviving same-sex partner? Where is the line between expressive speech and providing a service? Is it in the drawing? The baking? The decorating of a hotel bedroom? Is your right to free speech worth more than my right to equality? Is it about the message or is the medium also the message?

The cases discussed in this chapter underline why free speech has to be a queer-rights issue. We have to grasp it, and ensure that it is not used to undermine our fundamental rights to equality and non-discrimination.

Chapter 4
I Know a Place

One night in the flat in Chueca, I watched *Boys Don't Cry*. A blockbuster hit from the US starring Hilary Swank that came out in 1999. I decided to watch it on my own; there was something that told me this was not a popcorn gay male convoy kind of film. The film is a dramatisation of the real-life story of Brandon Teena. Brandon (Swank), a young trans man growing up in Humboldt, Nebraska, falls for a girl, Lana (Chloë Sevigny), who fancies him back. Brandon identifies as a guy (although of course we do not know how Brandon would identify today), and spoiler — the film ends with the beautiful young man being brutally raped and murdered.

I have only cried watching three films in my life, and this is one of them (the other two, if you are curious, are *Madame Butterfly*, the 1995 adaptation, and *Grave of the Fireflies*). I didn't just cry, I sobbed. I couldn't help but wonder: Why can't Brandon meet Lana and live happily ever after? Why is Brandon murdered? Where are the films about trans boys meeting girls and falling in love, having families, and living. Not dying, not being killed, but living and thriving. In many of the queer films we watched, the endings were deeply sad. Even in recent depictions of trans men, there is rape. I excitedly read Jeannette Winterson's book *Frankissstein* only to be shaken when the trans male romantic lead suffers a horrendous assault in a bathroom. Sexual assaults are presented to us as a probability in our lives.

When I watched *Boys Don't Cry* as a young person just coming out in the world, I recognised something of myself in Brandon. I mourned his death and understood the message. Brandon's transgression was lethal. It was dangerous. I was scared. For the first time, I felt that I had seen somebody on screen that I identified with, in the clothes he wore, the way he wanted to be intimate, his struggle to express his gender identity — but he was brutally punished for his authenticity and bravery. I sobbed because I was mourning for Brandon, but also for myself.

Other than Brandon, the only other trans male representation that I can remember seeing in my 20s was Max in *The L word*. But I didn't want to be Max. He was too queer, too strange, had sex with men and got pregnant. Everyone wanted to be Shane (that is, those of us masc of centre). Shane gets all the girls, Shane is with Carmen, she even got with Bette. I decided to stick with Shane, and I grieved and buried Brandon. I decided that my life would be easier if I tried to live it as a lesbian.

While I decided to push aside the growing understanding of my own genderqueerness, I couldn't quite let it go. I started to investigate queer and trans life expectancy and found that in some countries trans people could expect to live until their

30s. I wrote a letter in to *El País*, the largest Spanish national newspaper, for Pride 2010, calling for trans remembrance and advocating for trans rights. I wrote that trans people were dying young due to the combination of poverty and difficult life circumstances, that violence and murder were cutting trans life short.

In Nebraska, where Brandon lived and died, the criminalisation of sodomy was repealed in 1977. Same-sex activity was legal there way before it was in Texas. But changing criminal laws is just one part of the battle. The murder of Brandon Teena and Matthew Shepard five years later (as well as the murder of James Byrd Jr by avowed white supremacists) led to calls for hate-crime laws to be brought into place. In 2009, Barack Obama signed into law the *Matthew Shepard and James Byrd Jr Hate Crimes Prevention Act*, which expanded hate-crime legislation to include crimes motivated by a victim's actual or perceived gender, gender identity, or sexual orientation.

I do not believe in carceral feminism and do not believe that introducing more criminal laws, increasing jail sentences, or even putting people in jail is the answer to tackling homophobia or transphobia, but we do need legal measures to prevent the violence that women and queer people face. Today, young queer people continue to face bullying, harassment, and violence due to their gender, gender identity, and sexual orientation, and hate crimes are on the rise.

In June 2019, a photograph of the bloodied faces of two women on a date in London went viral after they were subjected to a homophobic attack after refusing to kiss on a bus home in Camden. The women were verbally and physically abused because of their sexuality. They were punched, called lesbians, and ended up in hospital with facial injuries. In March 2021, there was a national outcry during the pandemic when a young woman, Sarah Everard, was kidnapped in South London, assaulted, and murdered by a police officer. She was walking home when he kidnapped her. In February 2023, vigils were held across the UK and Ireland after a young trans girl, Brianna Ghey, was murdered. The outpouring of grief over her death showed solidarity and love with the trans community. These are just three examples of how women, regardless of their gender identity and sexual orientation, face violence every day just for being out in public. They are examples of how violence against women is the most pervasive human-rights violation in the world, and why we need to do more to protect all women from violence.

But it's not just women who are attacked — gay men, trans people, and genderqueer people face random and senseless acts of violence for transgressing gendered norms of dress and expression. Think of Travis Alabanza, who speaks about having a hamburger thrown at them on Waterloo Bridge along with a transphobic comment in 2016. In August 2023, two men were stabbed in a suspected homophobic attack outside the Two Brewers on Clapham High Street. This happened in the same month that two gay men were attacked coming home from Black Pride. According to the leading LGBTQ+ organisation in the UK, Stonewall, hate crimes based on sexual orientation are up 112 per cent in the last five years and 186 per cent for trans people. I could fill a whole book solely with the assaults, attacks, murders, and rapes committed against women and queer people. And those are just the reported crimes; we know most cases do not get reported.

At some point in my 20s, when I was dating women as a woman, I stopped going to straight bars. My girlfriend, a beautiful feminine woman, and I — well, a short half-Asian genderqueer nerd often mistaken for a teenage boy — would be constantly interrupted. Men in bars or even on the street would approach to try it on with my girlfriend, often drunk and menacing when they would see us together. We would leave the club to search for the safe space of a friend's apartment or a gay bar. At best, when you are out with a beautiful woman, men hit on your girlfriend and you are simply invisible to them. This still happens to me, all the time. At worst, things turn violent. It happens not even due to overt displays of affection, but simply because of the way we move, talk, dress, dance, or look. Because two women dare to be together and reject the male gaze.

Even when I was talking about writing this book, I was interrupted. I was in a gay bar in Geneva having a drink with Jen Robinson. We were deep in conversation about my coming-out story and the steps that I was taking to schedule top surgery. A straight man approached Jen as we sat together and would not leave her alone. He ignored her polite refusals and my requests to leave us be and to let us talk. The man would not leave. He persisted, moving his body closer, becoming more intrusive and aggressive. In the end, the barmen had to throw him out.

I was enraged. This was my safe space. A space I had picked to avoid this kind of unwanted behaviour. Jen thanked the barmen and said it was the first time in her experience that bar staff had acted so decisively to keep us feeling safe. This should not be the exception but the rule.

Toxic masculinity is exhausting. Queer spaces are a haven.

▲

Historically, queer people have gathered together to meet one another in an environment where we can feel safe. A place where the outside world of homophobia and prejudice can be left aside. A place where we are together and not alone. Rooms of anticipation, where new lovers and friendships are made. The law tried to deal with us by banning such association. In Miami in the 1950s, a 'one-homo-per-bar rule' meant that it was illegal for a bar owner to know that there were two or more gays congregated in the establishment. In New York, there was a ban on serving gay people in bars until the 1970s. The criminal laws existed to target the gays, while city by-laws were enacted to police the landowners and publicans. These were phased out in the US and UK, but the battle to establish queer spaces continues. This is extremely difficult in places where homosexuality is not legal or where criminal laws are used to silence and target activists.

In October 2022, two gay men were killed and a woman shot by a gunman who waited outside Tepláreň, a gay bar in Bratislava, Slovakia. Though Slovakia is part of the European Union, it doesn't recognise same-sex relationships in the law. A number of politicians have been peddling homophobic rhetoric. When the news of the shooting broke, I called my friend, a Slovak queer woman who lives in Bratislava, to check that she was okay. She had been there earlier that night and was devastated. The attack wasn't just about a bar, but about one of the only safe spaces that they had. It was an attack on their home.

That same year, the European Court of Human Rights decided the first case in international human-rights law concerning queer spaces. This case concerned a woman called Tsomak, who co-owned and managed a gay bar called the DIY in the centre of the Armenian capital, Yerevan. She gave press interviews highlighting the situation for LGBTQ+ people in her country and became subject to online hate campaigns, intimidation, and threats. People started to enter the bar to threaten and intimidate her. At 5.00 am on 8 May 2012, after weeks of receiving these threats, DIY was set on fire. A man was seen on the CCTV wearing a jacket with the logo of a group associated with neo-Nazis. He later bragged about the arson, saying that 'the club was a gathering place for LGBT persons who brought shame on Armenia' and that the bar was run by a lesbian who had participated in a pride march.

Following the attack, the front of the club was covered in homophobic graffiti, much of it personally attacking Tsomak. It warned her not to reopen the club or it would be attacked again. The hooligans also broke in and destroyed what was left of the inside of the club. They drew swastikas on the walls. The online attacks against her also intensified. Comments on Facebook, YouTube, and other platforms were posted stating that she 'should die', 'should be burnt', and should be 'put in an electric chair'. In public, Tsomak was continually attacked, abused, threatened, and spat at by men dressed in black fascist uniform. She was terrified.

On 17 May, a parliamentarian from the ruling party in Armenia gave an interview stating that the attacks against the DIY were welcome. He said, 'Sects and sexual deviants should be fought against by even more rigorous means … At the same time, I call on people to refrain from extreme actions …' This was soon followed by a statement from the Deputy Speaker of the National Assembly, who accused homosexuals of creating a 'den of perversion'. It wasn't only Tsomak and the queer community who were targeted. Her sister was also told to resign from her job, simply for being a family member of a lesbian. Tsomak and her sister left Armenia and applied for asylum in Sweden. They had been targeted and persecuted all because Tsomak had run a gay bar.

In 2022, ten years after the attacks, the European Court of Human Rights finally decided the case. Obtaining international justice is a long waiting game. The court's judgment was an important victory for Tsomak against the Armenian state. It underlines that 'treatment which is grounded upon a predisposed bias on the part of the heterosexual majority against a homosexual minority may, in principle, fall within the scope of Article 3'. Discriminatory treatment may, the court says, amount to degrading treatment. This is very important because Article 3 of the European Convention on Human Rights and its international legal equivalent under Article 7 of the International Covenant on Civil and Political Rights create an absolute prohibition on cruel, inhuman, and degrading treatment. These are non-derogable obligations, meaning that states can never violate this prohibition. Recognising that acts of homophobia and discriminatory treatment can cross the threshold as an affront to human dignity is thus a very important finding.

As part of the implementation of the judgment, Armenia has to draft a law on equality in line with international human-rights standards and take action to raise awareness about the discrimination and prejudice experienced by LGBTQ+ people. The state has to ensure that there is adequate training for law enforcement and criminal-justice practitioners and that hate crimes with homophobic motives are effectively investigated.

But the human-rights situation in Armenia remains extremely difficult. Queer people continue to face discrimination and violence. According to Pink Armenia, there were 50 hate-crime incidents in 2023.

Queer spaces are not only about physical space, but also about the building of community. My friend Aisling who lives in Dublin explained to me that when she first came out, she didn't know people to go out with. She was too shy to go to a bar on her own. So she bought a copy of *Gay Community News* and found a whole range of groups and activities for queer people in Dublin. There were groups for gay male hikers, Irish-language speakers, knitters, queer Narcotics Anonymous. As we sat in a pub in Dublin, she explained, 'So Luke always teases me — he says, "You're a joiner," and it's true. There is a queer group for literally everything, and even if you are in Mayo [outside of the capital] there is a monthly meet-up.'

Aisling joined two groups — one called Running Amach, which organised coffee meet-ups for lesbians and bi women so that they could make contact and go to bars together later. Aisling told me that 'amach' means 'around/out' in Irish, so the group used a lovely play on words. The other group was a lesbian and bi hockey club, Pink Ladies. Through joining clubs, Aisling built herself a queer community and met her girlfriend. She even claimed that Dublin now has a better scene for queer women than San Francisco or LA. Queer social enterprises, civil-society groups, pride groups within workplaces, and community initiatives all play a vital role in emphasising that LGBTQ+ people are not alone and that they have a support system.

I learnt about the importance of queer community when I moved from Ireland to London and found my own queer family. I grew up with them, into our queerness. It was during our 20s that many of us started to feel that we should also give back and fight for those who are more marginalised within the community, through different forms of activism. Some people decided to volunteer with homeless charities, others started campaigning to save queer spaces, and I decided to volunteer with an LGBTQ+ asylum and refugee charity.

I spent a year sifting through asylum claims, meeting asylum seekers and refugees from countries all over the world to write a report on how asylum claims based on sexual orientation and gender identity were being processed in the UK. I started working there two years after the Supreme Court decision of *HJ and HT v Home Secretary*, which concerned asylum claims brought by people who had been persecuted for reasons of homosexuality. Until this judgment, asylum seekers were simply told that they could go home and conceal their homosexuality and live discreetly in order to avoid being persecuted. When the two asylum seekers in this case, gay men from Iran and Cameroon, were told they could to go back and live in the closet, they challenged the dismissals of their asylum claims.

The court starts its judgment by noting the 'evil of persecution' that queer people face around the world due to religious extremism, and how gay people face the death penalty in some countries. The court states that LGBTQ+ rights are 'one of the most demanding social issues of our time', explaining that under the international Refugee Convention, people are entitled to protection when their governments refuse to protect them, or persecute them on the basis of their gender identity or sexual orientation. The Supreme Court affirms that the Refugee Convention should enable queer people to 'live freely and openly, without fearing that they may suffer harm of the requisite intensity or duration because they are ... gay'. The judges understood what the lower courts had failed to grasp, that someone's sexual identity is inherent to one's very identity as a person. In what is now a celebrated passage from the judgment, Lord Alan Rodger explains:

> In short, what is protected is the applicant's right to live freely and openly as a gay man. That involves a wide spectrum of conduct, going well beyond conduct designed to attract sexual partners and maintain relationships with them. To illustrate the point with trivial stereotypical examples from British society:

just as male heterosexuals are free to enjoy themselves playing rugby, drinking beer and talking about girls with their mates, so male homosexuals are to be free to enjoy themselves going to Kylie concerts, drinking exotically coloured cocktails and talking about boys with their straight female mates. *Mutatis mutandis* — and in many cases the adaptations would obviously be great — the same must apply to other societies. In other words, gay men are to be as free as their straight equivalents in the society concerned to live their lives in the way that is natural to them as gay men, without the fear of persecution.

For many of the asylum seekers and refugees who I met, this judgment was a game-changer for their asylum claims. We found that in many instances claimants were no longer obliged to conceal their sexuality to be successful. However, we also found that claims continued to be refused due to a culture of disbelief. LGBTQ+ claimants faced inappropriate and sexually explicit questioning, stereotyped assumptions about queer relationships, and difficulties proving their sexuality even when evidence was presented about relationships and sexual intimacy. It was a 'damned if you have it, damned if you don't' approach. Too much evidence and the asylum seekers were accused of being performative; too little and the claims were considered to be lacking in merit.

Specialised support groups are vital for these claimants. Refugees often escape their homes with no financial means of support and need to build a new network of friends and family. Queer support groups present them with a lifeline, a way to meet other people who have lived through similar experiences and who they can live openly with. Today, organisations such as African Rainbow Family play a vital role in supporting LGBTQ+ refugees and asylum seekers, offering services, housing support, and a community.

In London in any given year, you can go to Pride, Black Pride, ParaPride, Bi Pride, Trans+ Pride. You can hop on the train and go to Margate Pride or Brighton Pride. You might even venture abroad and go to Amsterdam Pride to see the colourful boats float along the canal with families out wearing pink, or to Madrid Pride, where millions descend on the capital to party into the early hours of the next day. Around the world, pride marches and pride events take place to mark the importance of recognising our rights. Pride is a significant event. I still clearly remember attending my first event in Paris, choosing my outfit (inspired by Shane from *The L Word*, baby-dyke style) and dancing all night in a lesbian bar in the Marais. It was fabulous. For many young queers, it is their first sight of the broad spectrum of rainbow lives — from jockstraps to families.

Today, there is a debate in countries like England about whether Pride has been co-opted, whether it has become too corporate. In Madrid, the massive Pride march bringing together millions of people takes place alongside Orgullo Crítico, which eschews corporate and mainstream visions of pride. Its alternative protest instead features immigrants, sex workers, queer families, and Black and ethnic minority groups who do not feel visible or represented in official pride marches that feature floats costing thousands of euros to parade. I like this choice, this flourishing of pride events. The more events, the better.

One of my friends, a prominent queer activist, described Pride as 'bullshit' when I told her I was writing about Pride as a human-rights issue. I understand the queer critiques, but Pride is not bullshit. It is a display of human rights and a visible reminder that we must continue to fight for equality.

Pride is extremely important in a context where queer people have been and continue to be excluded from other political and community causes. In many countries, it is the only time that a visible group of people come out to advocate specifically for LGBTQ+ rights. This might be in huge numbers such as in London or Madrid or it might be in very small numbers in countries like Sri Lanka. Regardless of how many people there are, the event is significant because queer people are marginalised and sidelined in society.

I was absolutely shocked to learn that in the US, a Supreme Court judgment exists that upholds the right of St Patrick's Day organisers to ban queer groups from marching in those parades. In the 1995 case of *Hurley v Irish-American Gay, Lesbian, and Bisexual Group of Boston (GLIB)*, the organisers, the South Boston Allied War Veterans Council refused to allow GLIB to express their pride in their Irish heritage and banned them from marching. The queer group challenged the ban on the basis that they were being discriminated against and that the veterans had no right to exclude them. But GLIB lost in the Supreme Court, meaning that pride groups have continued to be excluded from St Patrick's Day parades in different states in the US. It was only in 2024 that Staten Island in New York overturned its ban and held its first inclusive St Patrick's Day parade. The *Hurley* decision was recently cited as precedent in the *303 Creative* wedding-website case to deny services to gay couples.

In Europe, the battle to gather and hold pride marches remains very much ongoing. In 2022, President Aleksandar Vučić of Serbia announced that he was cancelling EuroPride, which was due to take place in September that year. Belgrade had competed with Barcelona, Dublin, and Lisbon to host the pan-European pride event. The organisers wanted to highlight the systematic discrimination that queer people face in the Balkans, but the government said that it was going to cancel the event because it offended family values. Other cancellations have taken place due to 'security reasons'. All are a breach of our fundamental human right to protest.

The European Court of Human Rights has repeatedly affirmed that banning pride parades violates our rights to free speech and equality. Some of the cases that have come before the court show not only how celebrations are prevented, but also how activists face horrendous abuse and violence when they celebrate.

In Georgia, queer activists in Tbilisi were assaulted during their march to mark the 2007 International Day Against Homophobia. Religious groups converged on the activists and threatened to burn them to death. The ECHR found in this case that the government violated protest rights as well as the absolute prohibition on cruel, inhuman, and degrading treatment due to the fear, anguish, and insecurity that the marchers experienced. Six years later on the same day, activists were attacked once again. Only 12 queer people had turned up to mark the 2013 International Day Against Homophobia, forming a silent flash mob in Pushkin Square. They soon found themselves surrounded by nearly 40,000 counter-demonstrators, who were chanting death threats and homophobic insults while brandishing wooden sticks and iron batons. Twelve queers versus a 40,000-strong mob. Shockingly, the ECHR found that far from protecting the activists, the government in fact connived in the acts of violence that the activists faced.

The ECHR has established again and again that countries have specific duties to prevent violence that is motivated by hatred. Article 11 of the European Convention on Human Rights protects the right to peaceful assembly and freedom of association. Along with the right to freedom of expression, it is one of the foundations of a democratic society. The court has explained that states have positive obligations to ensure that groups belonging to minorities, including the queer community, can exercise the right to protest and participate in activism for their causes, as unpopular as they may be in the country. States also have obligations to protect those who are protesting and organising peaceful assembly from attacks. This includes ensuring a safe and enabling environment for the right to peaceful assembly — including queer celebrations and events. In order for governments to comply with their human-rights obligations, state authorities must facilitate protest, demonstrations, and celebrations such as Coming Out Day or Pride. They must protect protestors from violence and counter-demonstrations and must ensure that activists do not fear harm or arrest from police officers.

Yet in many European countries, activists are not protected, violence is not prevented, and the legal system is complicit in criminalising queer people. International human-rights committees and courts have been particularly critical of Russia for banning pride marches and for failing to respect the rights of queer people to protest. ILGA-Europe, the European branch of the International Lesbian, Gay, Bisexual, Trans, and Intersex Association, ranks Russia as the least supportive country in Europe, placing it at the bottom of its annual survey of 49 European countries in 2013, 2014, and 2024. Russian authorities have consistently refused permits for pride parades, intimidated and detained activists, and tolerated anti-LGBTQ+ remarks from government figures. In one recent case, the ECHR found numerous human-rights violations when police arrested and detained those advocating for LGBTQ+ rights in Russia, preventing them from protesting while counter-demonstrators were allowed to hound and assault them with impunity.

Events such as Pride and celebrations against homophobia, biphobia, and transphobia are milestones. They are markers of how far we have come and how far we still have to go to ensure we all have human rights. We cannot take them for granted. Some countries are yet to ever hold a pride parade, while in others obtaining corporate and official sponsorship remains an important goal.

In 2024 in Japan, my friends told me that a major corporate lobby group, Keizai Doyukai, participated in

Tokyo Rainbow Pride for the first time. They were overjoyed, as most queer people in Japan still do not come out at work and some even pretend to be in heterosexual relationships. Business involvement is an important step in showing people that they can be their full selves inside and outside of the office. Nobody wants a capitalist corporate take-over of Pride, but the more facets of society we have celebrating our lives, the better.

The last few years when I have marched, I have done so to celebrate and to protest. I march for my 15-year-old self, who struggled to come out and who did not know then that I would one day be so happy in myself. I march for my 23-year-old self, who didn't know what would become possible for me in terms of my gender. I march for the rights that our queer elders have fought for and for those that we must continue to battle for. I raise my voice with all the other beautiful queers of the now expanded rainbow flag. I march alongside the queer asylum seekers, migrants, sex workers, and family collectives, the young and the old, the bull dykes and drag queens, bisexuals and trans and non-binary folks so that we can live in a world where we have equal rights. Where we can celebrate our personal and collective journey. To remind people that we are here and queer. And that we have a right to come together in queer spaces.

Chapter 5
Husbands and Wives

During the months of 2018 when I worked on Rosanna Flamer-Caldera's case, including the arguments on her right to a family life, I was in the process of starting my own rainbow family.

Growing up, I didn't know anyone in a queer family, and I didn't think it was a possibility for me. But during my first year working at the Bar, I started dating a woman who wanted to have a baby. She made it clear five years later, in the summer of 2015, when I flew to meet her in Almería in the south of Spain. She wanted to do it alone or with me — but either way, she wanted to have a baby. She was sure of her desire for motherhood, and I was sure of my desire to be with her. I had fallen for her quickly. She danced flamenco and my Japanese cousin called her 'Penélope Cruz'; she reminded *me* of one of the actresses from Almodóvar's movies. Smart, fiery, and feminist.

I had no idea how hard it would be for us to have

a child. How long it would take. How many injections, hormones, doctors' appointments, and disappointments. How it consumes your life. How you count the cycles. How there are apps for everything. I didn't know to consider all of this beforehand, because I simply didn't know about it. Maybe it was for the best, given how difficult fertility treatment is and how difficult it is for many queer people to have families.

In some ways, it was easy at first, or at least easier, because it wasn't my body, my cycles, my hormones, and my ovaries that were being manipulated. At first, it was G's journey. We hadn't worked the terms out. I was working full-time as a barrister in England and she was working full-time as a human-rights lawyer in Spain and we were trying to squeeze in fertility appointments around writing legal briefs. My head was filled with questions. What would it mean if G was pregnant? Would I legally be a co-parent? How would we parent? Where would we live? What would we tell our family and friends? Were we ready for parenthood? Was it okay for us to be accessing reproductive technologies when there were so many children in the world without a home and who could be fostered or adopted?

As the appointments progressed over the years, our relationship changed too. We decided that we wanted to co-parent the child. But although G and I were in a committed relationship, we had no official paperwork confirming this status.

Then one day as we sat in a public health clinic in Madrid, waiting to go through treatment, a doctor asked us a simple question. 'Are you married?' He barely looked up from the medical notes. 'No,' we said. 'Well, you probably should do it.' He looked up. 'Because right now, only G will be the parent.' We looked at each other in that small green windowless office. Two human-rights lawyers sitting in a doctor's room — silent, dumbfounded. We had proceeded on an assumption that since we were going through the process in a recognised public fertility clinic that we would both be recognised as the parents. Not so, back then in Madrid. According to the doctor, the law meant that two women could access fertility treatment but could only share their genetic material or both have parental recognition if a marriage had taken place. We were unsure if he was correct. So we decided to speak to an expert.

I called a lawyer friend of mine. 'Get married,' she said. 'It's the only way to protect both your positions and avoid having to go through an adoption process.' I thanked her and told G. We should get married, I suggested. My follow up was: Should we challenge this in court? Why should queer people have to be married for both to be on the birth certificate and be recognised as parents? If we were a straight couple accessing IVF, there would be no requirement to be married or in a civil union. If we were heterosexual, we could sign up as an unmarried couple.

I knew the answer to the litigation question even before I asked it. We didn't have time to litigate the case. It was G's biological clock rather than legal principle that would ultimately determine the answer to this question. We didn't have time to bring a case that would wind its way through the court system for years and be extremely costly. We had to get moving fast because G was about to turn 40 and, in the Spanish public health system, treatment was only available to women in their 30s. Also, being a litigant would add another level of stress to the already stressful journey of going through fertility treatment.

We decided to get married — to celebrate our relationship and love, but also to access the treatment that we needed. And I did not want to have to go through an adoption process if G had a baby. I had in my mind the experience of my friend Madeleine Rees, who after nearly 16 years was still going through the process of adopting her daughter. There was also another very practical reason to get married. I wanted to be able to donate my eggs to G in a procedure called the ROPA method (reception of oocytes from the partner). It is a form of shared motherhood where one person provides the egg and the other gestates the embyro. We needed to be married to do this as non-anonymous egg donation is against the law in Spain. A civil partnership was not enough for Spanish law at the time. So we decided to get married, and quickly. The law left us with no option.

At the beginning of 2019, gay marriage was not available in Northern Ireland where I grew up, so our choices of wedding location were Madrid or London. Our decision was based on paperwork: London required the least documentation and no translation of documents. Spain required everything to be translated, stamped, and notarised with ceremonial procedure at great expense. Pragmatism won the day. We called the registry office and got a date, and then we called our families and told them that we were getting married in three months' time.

The wedding took place on a Friday in March in Marylebone Town Hall. We threw a bouquet as if it were a grenade of love. My friend Bernard caught it. He later proposed to his girlfriend on the canal in Hackney. I saw him leap for those flowers.

We walked from the town hall down to Seymour Place and turned the corner to Crawford Street into a pub with our friends and some family. On that short walk, I thought about all the people who would still deny us this legal paperwork, this ritual and union, and with it the associated legal protections. And, of course, the transcendent dimensions — a union recognised by international human-rights law as the foundation of family and even the nation. I also thought about the people and governments, like the Holy See, who use their time and energy at the United Nations and around the world to advocate against marriage equality. The people who make queer people feel lesser, who would hide us away in a closet rather than let us burst forth with celebration and joy. And I thought of all the people who have fought for our rights throughout the decades so that we could get married. These are things that we cannot take for granted.

After dinner at the pub, we went to a karaoke place in central London. Most of G's friends are Spanish and sang camp songs like 'Todos Me Miran' and 'A Quién le Importa', anthems of the queer community in Spain and Latin America that I had learnt in Madrid in my early 20s. As the 30 or so friends shouted the words to the songs, I was transported back to a drag bar in Mexico nearly ten years beforehand. It was the year that I had met G and first fallen for her. It was also the year I met the Chilean trail-blazer who would teach me how important it is that we gain legal recognition of our queer relationships. Her name is Karen Atala Riffo.

I met Karen in 2010 in the town of Cuernavaca, Mexico, where I was helping to organise a training session for judges of the Mexican Supreme Court. The training session on gender equality was scheduled over Pride and involved a gathering of legal experts from Latin America to discuss emerging trends in case law concerning women's rights and LGBTQ+ rights. Karen was invited as a judge from Chile to talk about her own case. We sat in a large seminar room with judges and their clerks all day in the heat discussing case law.

Karen told us about the discrimination she faced in Chile due to her sexuality. She had lost the care and custody of her three daughters and also lost her job as a judge, all because she came out as a lesbian after she got divorced. Karen had been married to a man called Ricardo, and they had three daughters together. An amicable custody agreement was reached when they separated in March 2002. But on 14 January 2003, Ricardo filed a lawsuit against Karen, stating that she was 'not capable of watching over and caring for' their children given 'her new sexual lifestyle choice, together with her cohabiting relationship with another woman'. Ricardo and his lawyers argued that to 'treat as normal, within the legal order, partners of the same sex' would 'distort the meaning of a human couple, man and woman, and therefore, alters the natural meaning of the family'. They argued the children would be under constant risk of contracting sexually transmitted diseases such as herpes and HIV given 'the sexual practices of lesbians'.

The court in Chile granted provisional custody to Ricardo and regulated Karen's visits with the children. The judge held that arguments based on the wellbeing of children take on great importance, which the judge interpreted in a heterosexist and prejudiced way 'in the context of a heterosexual and traditional society'.

On 8 May 2003, a family court in Villarrica granted custody of the children to Ricardo on the grounds of Karen's sexuality. One of the primary reasons was because Karen was living with her girlfriend. Karen had no choice but to battle her way through the legal system. A year later, she lost her case before the Supreme Court of Chile, meaning that she lost the custody of her children. The court's prejudice is palpable. It concluded among other things that Karen had decided to put her own interests before those of her children because she had chosen to live with a woman and that 'the potential confusion over sexual roles that could be caused in them by the absence from the home of a male father and his replacement by another person of the female gender poses a risk to the integral development of the children from which they must be protected'. If you are confused by those words, it is because the reasoning is baffling. The Supreme Court decided that children would be better off without their mother because their mother was living with another woman. The court placed the 'potential confusion over sexual roles' at the apex of their worries.

I think for most parents there is nothing worse than losing custody over your children. Not being able to see them and care for them. I can't imagine the pain. When Karen talked about her own situation and the legal prejudice she had suffered, a hush came over the room. If the law could do this to a judge, what could it do to the rest of us?

When I met Karen, she had already lodged her legal appeal before a regional human-rights body, the Inter-American Court of Human Rights. As a lawyer at Women's Link Worldwide, I'd worked on an amicus brief that had been submitted in support of her case. She was now awaiting the court's decision.

The Inter-American Court is my favourite human-rights court. It gives long, well-reasoned decisions and orders states to make reparations that are often systemic and not simply individual. It is the only human-rights court that has made it clear that gay people have a right to marry under international human-rights law, even if states have ignored such calls to recognise it. But in the case of a mother who has lost custody of her children, what can such a court do? The decisions before international and regional human-rights courts take years if not decades to resolve. Yet once the decision is handed down, it is binding.

After a full day of legal seminars, we were ready for a drink. After dinner with the participants, who were mostly well-established, older lawyers and judges from across Latin America, Karen and I identified each other as 'playing on the same team' and went out to find a gay bar. We didn't have smartphones back then, so we asked around on the street where we might find some Pride celebrations. I was mildly terrified. It was pitch black and I was in a foreign country. I asked Karen if she thought it was safe to be asking random people in the street, in the dark, in a town we did not know where we could find a gay bar, but she told me 'securitisation is a capitalist concept' and that we would be fine. We found a bar, Enigma, and got treated to some of the best drag shows I've seen.

Sitting in that bar with Karen, with drag queens singing 'Todos Me Miran' by Gloria Trevi, I came to understand how the law that should be there to protect us can be used instead to deny us our most fundamental rights: our rights to form and grow families, to care for our children, to protect them, to form social relationships, and to seek self-fulfilment as individuals, lovers, partners, and parents. These rights should be protected regardless of our sexuality. Yet Karen had been separated from her children by the legal system because she dared to fall in love with a woman.

On 24 February 2012, nine years after her loss of custody, Karen won her case, with the Inter-American Court of Human Rights affirming that any regulation, act, or practice that is discriminatory and based on a person's sexual orientation is prohibited. The court made it clear that arguments based on a mother's sexual orientation — or unfounded and stereotyped assumptions about parental capacity and suitability to promote a child's wellbeing because of sexuality — are inappropriate in law. Prejudiced arguments are often made that it is in the child's best interests to have contact only with a heterosexual parent. The court rejects this and makes it clear that the child's best interests cannot be used as a reason to justify discrimination against queer parents. In other words, what is in the child's bests interests is to be with their parent or parents who love them — regardless of sexuality.

Karen set a global precedent. She became a leading figure calling for marriage equality in Chile and has fought for trans identity and anti-discrimination laws. She was reinstated as a judge. Her case shone a light on the practice of family courts around the world: many states continue to force gay people to choose between being able to fall in love with their partner of choice and being able to raise their children. Denying children the right to be raised, and loved, by their queer parents denies children the right to family life and love. It is a travesty of justice.

In the excellent book *We Are Family*, Susan Golombok, professor of child development at the University of Cambridge, explains that at the end of the 1970s not a single lesbian who had fought for custody of her children in the UK courts had won.

Constance Debré's book *Love Me Tender* highlights the ongoing custody battles that lesbians fight in France including her own.

In 2021, the European Court of Human Rights decided the case of a Polish woman (X) who was in a custody battle with her ex-husband after she started having a relationship with another woman (Z). It was, in fact, her own bloody parents who did not accept her sexuality and instituted proceedings to seek custody of her children. Courts initially granted the grandparents the custody application before deciding to grant full parental rights to the father on the basis that X 'doesn't want to abandon [her] excessive intimacy with Z in order to improve [her] relations with [her children]'. The courts ignored that she had been the main carer for the four children and that her ex-husband had not spent much time with them. After they split, he had barely used his contact rights with them. The ex-husband even said in court that X should retain custody of the youngest child, who was three years old.

The courts in Poland gave the mother a choice: she could continue to exercise her parental rights if she 'corrected her attitude' and left her girlfriend. The psychological experts and the judges all made references to her lifestyle and 'homosexuality' to reach their conclusions. The national court in Poland stated that 'the issue of raising a child in a same-sex relationship was very controversial' and that it was important that the youngest child, a boy, had a male role model in his life. The court ignored that X had never tried to stop her ex-husband from seeing the child.

She appealed the Polish courts' prejudiced decision and brought her case to the European Court of Human Rights. The ECHR condemned Poland and found that the mother's sexuality was 'omnipresent at every stage of the judicial proceedings' and that the courts in Poland had decided 'solely or decisively on consideration regarding her sexual orientation'. It found a violation of her rights to family life and non-discrimination.

Recently, the ECHR reached a similar decision in relation to a trans woman in Russia who lost custody of her children due to her transition. The court held that this had violated her family rights.

These cases, fought over years and sometimes decades, with significant distress to the mothers, are significant in making it clear that sexual orientation cannot be a reason to remove a child from the care of a parent and that when this is the sole reason it is contrary to international law. These cases illustrate the struggles that queer people have when they come out after conceiving children in heterosexual relationships. Many people decide to wait and come out once their children are over 18 years of age due to fears that their children will be removed.

When I told my American friend, a fellow queer parent, about the prejudice in the family courts, she suggested we watch a film called *Temblores* by Jayro Bustamante. The 2019 film depicts the social and religious pressures faced by a married father, Pablo, when he falls for another man in Guatemala. He risks losing his job, his children, his family, and his whole community for being gay. He ends up submitting to conversion therapy so that he can continue to see his children. He feels like he has no choice but to renounce his sexuality and his love. It is devastating. We sat in silence after the film, the prejudice weighing heavy on our hearts. Queer people should not feel lucky to live in a country where we can be recognised as the legal parents of our children. It should be the standard everywhere.

Underlying these cases and situations is the lack of recognition of same-sex relationships and state prejudice against queer people and their love. Same-sex relationships have for too long been seen by the family-court judges to be damaging and abnormal. This is why fighting for marriage equality and equal recognition of queer relationships has been a goal of the queer community.

There is debate among people in the queer community about whether energy and advocacy should go into fighting for gay marriage, essentially a conservative and assimilationist objective, rather than a goal of queer liberation. This is a long-standing debate. Back in the late 1980s and early 1990s, lesbians and gay men attended meetings in London where this issue was fiercely discussed during the AIDS crisis. Some felt that marriage equality was a distraction from more important goals such as healthcare, while others argued that it was vitally important to ensure that queers could enter hospitals and that their loved ones could inherit assets when they passed.

G and I talked about this in the lead-up to our wedding day. She believed that marriage is a patriarchal institution and one that feminists should reject and problematise. I was more romantic or perhaps traditional in my outlook and felt like marriage was important symbolically for queer people in order for our relationships to be granted the same recognition and status as heterosexual relationships.

The fact is that marriage equality plays an important role in protecting legal rights. Whether you want to get married or not, if something is available for heterosexuals then it should be available for us homos. Otherwise, it is straight-up discrimination. We should have the same choice as to whether we say *I do* or *I don't*.

Legal arguments against marriage equality echo Roger Miller's lyrics in the song 'Husbands and Wives' that 'pride is the chief cause in the decline / In the number of husband and wives'. Although Miller was talking about another kind of pride, it sums up the argument made by government lawyers around the world that the extension of marriage to queers will undermine the institution of marriage.

While international law enshrines the right of heterosexuals to get married, it does not recognise gay marriage as a right. As it stands, the Inter-American Court of Human Rights is the only international legal body that has recognised that there is a right to marriage equality. The court made human-rights history in 2017 when it explained in an advisory opinion that:

> States must ensure full access to all the mechanisms that exist in their domestic laws, including the right to marriage, to ensure the protection of the rights of families formed by same-sex couples, without discrimination in relation to those that are formed by heterosexual couples ...

The European Court of Human Rights has decided that countries must provide for some form of same-sex partnership recognition, such as civil partnerships, but that there is no human right to gay marriage. The right to marriage enshrined in the European Convention on Human Rights has been interpreted as only applying to heteros. The ECHR has held that it is a 'legislator's choice not to allow same sex marriage — a choice not condemnable under the Convention'. In Europe, marriage equality is still a right to be fought for.

At the time of writing, only 32 countries globally have legalised gay marriage and most of these countries are in Western Europe and Central and South America. Most countries that do have gay marriage have legislated for it, meaning that politicians have passed a law. But there are other ways that countries have ushered in gay marriage, such as national court cases and referenda. It is through national movements that gay marriage has come about rather than through international human-rights litigation.

Often the road to marriage equality starts with the introduction of civil partnerships. The rationale behind these legal arrangements is to provide queers some recognition but not grant us the full right to marriage. Separate but equal, as they say. Often this recognition comes with all the responsibilities but not all the rights of heterosexual marriage. My friend Madeleine Rees was in a civil partnership with her partner when they had their daughter. This granted them some legal recognition, but it did not grant them both parental rights.

In November 2023, I was in Geneva with Madeleine when she excitedly told me that the process to adopt her teenage daughter was finally going through. Although Madeleine and her partner were in a civil partnership in the UK and went to a fertility clinic together back in 2006, Madeleine is not on the birth certificate of her daughter. This is because when the UK government passed the legislation on civil partnerships, it did not grant automatic parental rights to the non-gestational mother. Madeleine got an order from the High Court, which gave her parental responsibility but not the full rights that would automatically come from being on the birth certificate. Parental responsibility was obviously necessary and important. It allowed Madeleine to prove she was her child's parent at school or when travelling with her, but it didn't allow Madeleine to pass on her British nationality to her daughter.

So all those years later Madeleine was finally formally adopting her own 16-year-old daughter. Madeleine's situation goes to show the lack of harmonisation between laws and the hidden differences that can exist between civil partnership and marriage arrangements. It should never have been this way. Madeleine should have been on her daughter's birth certificate from the get-go, recognised as one of the two mothers of their child.

Civil partnerships are not enough. They entrench difference when they are only available to queers and not to straight couples. As the South African Constitutional Court, one of the first courts to play a role in bringing about gay marriage, has explained:

> The exclusion of same-sex couples from ... marriage ... represents a harsh if oblique statement by the law that same-sex couples are outsiders ... that their need for affirmation and protection of their intimate relations as human beings is somehow less than that of heterosexual couples ... that their capacity for love, commitment and accepting responsibility is by definition less worthy of regard than that of heterosexual couples.

When I got married, it was important to me to marry rather than get a civil partnership. It was a statement of commitment and love, but also a political statement. I wanted to marry because in my own hometown in Northern Ireland it was still not available.

After my American friend, Luke, and I left the Oscar Wilde museum, we had a few hours before we had to get to the Abbey Theatre, where we were going to see a play. We were giving the American the full Dublin experience, so we decided to stop off at a pub, and Luke suggested we go to Grogan's, one of his favourites. He also wanted us to meet up with our mutual friend Aisling — the joiner.

In Grogan's, we settled down at one of the small tables inside over some Guinness and wine. As we caught up on each other's news, I told Aisling that I had split from G. She asked me if we had been married and I said that we had. I didn't know it, but both Aisling and the American had been actively involved in canvassing and advocating for marriage equality, in Ireland and the US. Both had rather unique experiences of being involved in referendum campaigns, and the discussion turned to their experiences of activism.

In 2015, the Republic of Ireland made legal history when it became the first country in the world to legalise gay marriage by way of a referendum. The referendum was a culmination of years of campaigning by individuals. When I was at Trinity, the campaign was led by activists including Katherine Zappone, who had married her wife in Canada and was trying to get her marriage recognised in Ireland. The two women had been together since 1981 and exchanged 'life partnership vows' with each other in 1982. They had been waiting to get married since those vows, and finally did so when a court case made same-sex marriage available in the province of British Columbia in 2003. Katherine wanted to get married because she loved Anne

Louise, but she was also concerned about pension provision, tax, and what would happen if one of them passed away.

In 2006, she brought a legal challenge in Ireland asking the courts to recognise her Canadian marriage, but the courts rejected her case. We were all crestfallen, but the campaigning continued, with Ireland introducing civil partnership in 2010. This was a step in the right direction, but Irish people wanted to get married. Change was in the air, and Ireland was throwing off the vestiges and grip of the Catholic Church.

In 2015, this change was finally happening, with the government announcing a national referendum on gay marriage. Aisling told us how she got involved in the grassroots campaign to usher in marriage equality by going door to door, walking with women and their babies around parks, and sitting in people's living rooms, coming out to absolute strangers to explain on a personal level what marriage equality would mean to her. She also took the opportunity to come out to her grandmother.

The marriage-equality campaign understood how important it was for queer people and allies to tell personal stories. It was not about sex. It was about equality. It was about love. For some people, these encounters were the first time they would knowingly meet a queer person, let alone have one in their living room. Aisling and her friends wanted to show them that queer people were everywhere and were 'normal people'. Neighbours, family members, parents, and colleagues.

The strategy worked. The referendum passed with a great majority, and Irish queers at home and abroad cheered. Dublin Castle was lit up with the rainbow colours, and people honked their horns as they drove past.

The referendum on gay marriage ushered in a new Ireland, one that is now very different from the one Aisling, Luke, and I grew up in. Dublin is maybe even more gay than San Francisco (it has more lesbian bars, if that's the barometer). With the yes vote in Ireland, 'we all came out of the closet and Ireland came out of the closet,' Aisling recalled. And it hasn't looked back since. The referendum was followed some years later by the Repeal the 8th campaign, which overturned the prohibition on abortion in Ireland.

I left Ireland when I was a student because I felt alienated by a country that didn't recognise queer relationships or women's rights to bodily autonomy, but I increasingly feel the tug of it, as home, a place that's welcoming for all Irish citizens, regardless of our sexuality, gender identity, or perhaps even race. I was proud to be showing my American friend this new Ireland, with all its queerness and bodily autonomy, especially as the US was lurching in the opposite direction.

My American friend, who had been patiently listening to us discussing Irish transformation, then shared her referendum story. I had no idea that she was in a domestic partnership with her partner when she decided to get involved in grass-roots campaigning. In California, there were civil partnerships for gay people but not marriage equality. But she wanted to get married, so she proposed to her girlfriend. She told us how the domestic-partnership legislation made sure that she had all the responsibilities that a marriage brings — for example, she would have been responsible for her partner's debts — but it did not grant them all the rights of a married couple. The partnership was also not recognised outside of the State of California, which meant that they were strangers in the eyes of the law if they drove to New Mexico or Texas, only a few hours away. In fact, queer people in domestic partnerships did not receive any of the 1,138 rights and benefits granted to married couples under federal law.

In 2008, the year my friend got engaged, California was fighting a fierce legal and political battle over gay marriage. A Supreme Court of California decision had declared that gay people should be able to get married. In response to this, conservative forces organised a referendum. The question, Proposition 8, did not ask if gay people should be allowed to marry. Instead, it asked Californians if they wanted to ban gay marriage.

Like Aisling in Ireland, the American went door to door in Los Angeles speaking to potential voters in order to get them to vote no to Prop 8. 'I dressed like a babe,' she told us, and she talked to complete strangers about how she was queer. Like Aisling, she would explain to people on their doorsteps why the initiative was harmful on a personal level. She talked and campaigned from her heart and shared how she wanted to marry her girlfriend.

When the Prop 8 referendum took place in 2008, the world was a different place to how it is now or even how it would be in 2015 when the Irish referendum took place. Though California is one of the most liberal states in the US, there were barely any actors or actresses who were open about their sexuality. My friend recalled how Rachel Maddow and

Ellen DeGeneres were on TV but neither of them really talked about their sexualities at the time she got engaged to her girlfriend. It was still rare to see a gay couple kiss on screen. Even Democratic politicians were not openly in favour of gay marriage.

After canvassing votes, the Prop 8 ballot took place on 4 November 2008. This is a significant date in US history as it was also the day of the US presidential election between Barack Obama and John McCain. The Prop 8 results were announced at the same time that America learnt that it had a new president: Barack Obama. This was a watershed moment in American politics, with the first Black president voted into the White House. Moments later, on the chyron running along the bottom of the screen of televisions across the US, my American friend learnt that the people of her state had voted to prevent her from having the right to marry. She told us how she had first been crying out of happiness at the monumental and historic news that her country had elected a person of colour to be president, but this then turned into tears of shock at the outcome of Prop 8: 'It felt like the state had turned its back on the gays.'

This juxtaposition between Obama getting elected and the Prop 8 outcome was a difficult moment for the queer community in California. How California goes, the rest of the US follows, my friend explained. In other words, the rest of the US states were watching carefully. If gay marriage could be banned in California, many Americans felt it could be banned elsewhere and maybe everywhere. Prop 8 resulted in an amendment to the California Constitution providing that only marriage between a man and a woman was valid and recognised in California.

After the Prop 8 referendum, two same-sex couples in California who wanted to get married decided to challenge the marriage ban, in a case that is now known as *Hollingsworth v Perry*. It was originally called *Perry v Schwarzenegger*, because Mr Terminator was the governor of California at the time. The couples won in the lower courts, which found that Prop 8 violated the Equal Protection clause of the constitution because it served no purpose other than 'to impose on gays and lesbians, through the public law, a majority's private disapproval of them and their relationships'. Although, as my American friend pointed out, the majority's disapproval in California was far from private — they had made their disapproval very public through the referendum.

The case was appealed to the US Supreme Court on 31 July 2012. I remember following the case at the time closely from the Hague, where I was interning at the Office of the Prosecutor of the International Criminal Court. The Hague is a hub of international justice, gathering lawyers from around the world. And alongside the prosecutions of war criminals, lawyers spent hours discussing the *Perry* case and whether it would lead to a landmark US precedent on marriage equality. A particular talking point was the strategy behind the case, as the gay couples had hired Ted Olson, the former solicitor-general of the US under George W. Bush and assistant attorney-general under Ronald Reagan. He was a well-known Republican and conservative who was now arguing a marriage-equality case. Our discussions were followed by nights out in the bars of the Hague, where it seemed 'Call Me Maybe' was played on repeat.

A year after filing the appeal, the Supreme Court handed down judgment on 26 June 2013, during Pride Month. It found that the opponents of gay marriage didn't have the standing to challenge the Californian Supreme Court's decision upholding the right to gay marriage. This outcome meant that same-sex marriage was now available in California. Following the Supreme Court decision, Kristin Perry and Sandy Stier, one of the two gay couples involved in the case, were married by the Californian attorney-general at the time, Kamala Harris, who later became the first woman of colour to be vice-president of the United States.

The *Perry* decision was important for Californians and brought a lot of publicity to the issue of marriage equality, but it did not go beyond California. It would take another two US Supreme Court cases to establish a right to marriage equality in the US Constitution, thus binding all the states within the United States of America. But we didn't have time in Grogan's to discuss those cases. Draining the last of our drinks, we had to say goodbye to Aisling and head quickly down William Street, past the statue of Molly Malone, the front gates of Trinity, and over the bridge to the North Side, where we were about to witness Marina Carr's play about a marriage ripped apart.

The legal arguments in *Perry* ended up being heard one day apart from another US Supreme Court case concerning marriage equality, called *United States v Windsor*. I found it curious that the Supreme Court had decided to hear two marriage-equality cases back-to-back; maybe they really wanted to say something about gay marriage. While I had followed *Perry* closely from the Hague, I was less familiar with *Windsor*. This is perhaps because the case concerned a piece of federal legislation, binding on all the states, signed into law by Bill Clinton in 1996.

The *Defense of Marriage Act (DOMA)* banned federal recognition of same-sex marriage by defining marriage as a union between a man and a woman. At the time the law was passed, there was no same-sex marriage anywhere in the country, but conservative groups were organised and got in ahead to prevent it from happening. The federal ban had major consequences. It swept over 1,000 federal statutes, impacting people's taxes and health benefits, and stopped queer couples from being recognised by the state even in death.

The *Windsor* case concerned two women, Edith Windsor and Thea Spyer, a New York couple who started dating in 1965. The two women got engaged in 1967 and waited all their lives to get married, finally tying the knot in Toronto in 2007. Thea was quadriplegic and sadly died soon after the marriage due to health complications. *DOMA* meant that Edith received an estate tax following Thea's death amounting to hundreds of thousands of dollars. If Thea and Edith had been in a straight marriage, Edith would not have had to pay a penny, since there is an estate-tax exemption for surviving spouses. It didn't matter that Thea and Edith were married in Canada or in a domestic partnership in New York. *DOMA* excluded same-sex couples from being defined as a spouse, effectively making them strangers in the eyes of the law.

On 9 November 2010, Edith filed her legal challenge in the New York courts, seeking a declaration that *DOMA* was unconstitutional. The district court and the US Court of Appeals for the Second Circuit both found the legislation to be unconstitutional. The battle then went to the US Supreme Court. As the lawyers got ready for the Supreme Court case, another important event occurred. New York passed its laws to allow for gay marriage. Now there was a state where gay marriage was available — but federal legislation was stopping queers from having equal benefits to heterosexual couples.

I spoke to US lawyer Roberta Kaplan, who argued this case before the Supreme Court. It was a January evening in 2024 when we talked, and she had just won a case representing E. Jean Carroll, who sued former president Donald Trump for defamation after she accused him of sexual assault and he stated that she wasn't his type. The court awarded Carroll $83.3 million in damages after Trump suggested she had made up the story to sell copies of a book. Roberta has been one of the main lawyers arguing marriage-equality cases in the US. She lives and works in New York, has impeccable blow-dried hair, and seems motherly in her tone before you remember that she is a Supreme Court advocate. She is out and proud and is married with a son.

Roberta had a personal connection to the *Windsor* case, since Thea had been her therapist when she was a young lesbian. Thea had helped her to come out and be proud, and years later Roberta had a chance to help Thea's wife, Edith, and to make legal history.

DOMA discriminated on the basis of sexuality. As Roberta puts it, *if Thea had been Theo, there would have been no discrimination and no tax bill.* The case was significant, Roberta explained, because 'marriage is the mechanism by which the legal system recognises our relationships with the people we love'. What made it even more compelling is that *DOMA* refused to recognise marriages even when states like New York allowed gay marriage. As the majority of the Supreme Court put it, 'DOMA seeks to injure the very class New York seeks to protect.' By 2013, 12 states provided for same-sex marriage, allowing queer couples to, in the words of Justice Anthony Kennedy, 'live with pride in themselves and their union and in a status of equality with all other married persons'. The case simply wanted to make sure that these gay marriages were recognised equally in federal law.

The Supreme Court handed down its judgment three years after it was filed, on 26 June 2013, the same day as *Perry*. The Supreme Court decided that *DOMA* deviated from the usual rule that definitions of marriage were to be decided on a state level, not by the federal government. The legislation, the court found, created a 'second-tier marriage', which was demeaning to married New York couples. The court also importantly found that *DOMA* impacted rainbow families:

> it humiliates tens of thousands of children now being raised by same-sex couples. The law in question makes it even more difficult for the children to understand the integrity and closeness of their own family and its concord with other families in their community and in their daily lives.

The court also pointed out that children were harmed by the legislation in a practical way, since it raised the cost of healthcare for same-sex families and reduced benefits to same-sex families. The court ultimately found that *DOMA* was unconstitutional because it had no legitimate purpose other than to injure and demean queer people who sought to marry or who had married. In making this finding, the court held that the Act violated basic Due Process and Equal Protection principles protected by the Constitution.

This was a watershed judgment, paving the way for marriage equality in the United States. But a different challenge needed to be mounted. *Windsor* ensured that the marriages in states that already recognised them were fully recognised at a federal level — but it did not discuss whether states had to offer gay marriage or whether states could continue to ban gay marriage. America was divided; liberal states had passed marriage-equality legislation, while conservative states continued to ban gay marriage. The fight had to continue.

It was exactly two years later, on 26 June 2015, that the Supreme Court decided another marriage-equality case, *Obergefell v Hodges*. This followed judicial decisions in Canada, South Africa, and Brazil, all finding that there was a constitutional right to marriage. Once again, the majority opinion was handed down by Justice Kennedy during Pride Month. In a 5–4 majority opinion, the court found in favour of a group of same-sex couples who had sued the states of Ohio, Michigan, Kentucky, and Tennessee for their refusal to recognise gay marriages. These states all defined marriage as a union between one man and one woman. The couples argued that the ban affected their right to liberty and to marry on the same basis as heterosexual couples.

The circumstances and lives of the couples bringing the case underline how important marriage is to people. The court heard how James Obergefell from Ohio met his partner John Arthur two decades before the court case. They fell in love, establishing a lasting, committed relationship. Arthur got sick in 2011. The couple wanted to get married before he died, but it wasn't available in Ohio, so they had to travel to Maryland to get married. The judgment details that 'it was difficult for Arthur to move, and so the couple were wed inside a medical transport plane as it remained on the tarmac in Baltimore. Three months later, Arthur died.' Obergefell brought his case to court because Ohio did not recognise his marriage from Maryland; it did not allow Obergefell to be listed as Arthur's surviving spouse on the death certificate. The judgment explains that 'By statute, they must remain strangers even in death, a state-imposed separation Obergefell deems "hurtful for the rest of time"'. He brought the case so that he could be listed as Arthur's surviving partner on the death certificate.

April DeBoer and Jayne Rowse, two other co-plaintiffs in the case, have an equally compelling story. The lesbian couple, both nurses, fostered and adopted a baby and then welcomed two other children into their life. One of the children requires around-the-clock care after being abandoned. Another has special needs. The two women from Michigan brought the case because that state did not recognise same-sex marriage and, the court notes, 'were tragedy to befall either DeBoer or Rowse, the other would have no legal rights over the children she had been permitted to adopt'. The couple brought the case to protect the legal rights of their children.

Each of the 14 couples in the case explained why marriage is practically and symbolically significant to their lives and the Supreme Court agreed with them and found that the US Constitution protects marriage equality. States cannot ban gay marriage, nor can they refuse to recognise marriages celebrated in another state. The court explains in its lofty language that excluding queer people from marriage is demeaning since 'Same-sex couples, too, may aspire to the transcendent purposes of marriage and seek fulfillment in its highest meaning.'

The judgment tackles head on many of the arguments used to deny people the right to same-sex marriage. These include:

- that marriage has always been a union between a man and a woman
- that allowing homosexuals to marry will undermine the institution of marriage
- that it is a politically sensitive matter and the proper institution to deal with this topic is the legislature
- that marriage is a religious institution
- that the purpose of marriage is for heterosexual procreation.

The court's judgment is clear that gay marriages do not undermine heterosexual marriages or the institution of marriage more generally. Allowing two men or two women to marry does not impact what heterosexual people do. Many heterosexual people do not marry to have children, and in any event queer people have children too. It importantly recognises that the right to marriage protects the rights of children, since it provides 'powerful confirmation from the law itself that gays and lesbians can create loving, supportive families', thus reflecting the reality that hundreds and thousands of children are already being raised in queer families.

The court held that the lack of recognition of gay marriage imposed stigma and injury, which is prohibited under the Constitution and was a grave and continuing harm to queer people who have been historically discriminated against. A denial of same-sex marriage is disrespectful and subordinates gay people to heterosexual people. It diminishes our personhood and disparages our choices. The court held that the right to marry is a fundamental right and that queer people cannot be deprived of this right and liberty.

The court's judgment underlines that the past alone cannot rule the present, and that past discrimination, which included criminalisation and banning gay people from government employment, cannot be relied upon to continue to oppress and deny people fundamental constitutional rights. The legal decision shows how concepts such as marriage evolve to be more inclusive, especially in a country that once also banned interracial marriages.

The US story is part of the global movement towards ensuring that queer people in love everywhere have the same rights as heterosexuals to marry, to have their marriages recognised by the state, and to obtain the protections that come with this. Couples who simply want to marry are bringing legal challenges and fighting for change all around the world.

A year after the US Supreme Court decision, the Constitutional Court of Colombia handed down its decision bringing in marriage equality in that country. My Colombian friend and colleague got married soon after and was able to buy a house with his husband since they were finally able to obtain a mortgage together. The Colombian court looked at comparative laws and jurisprudence, including the *Obergefell* decision, to conclude that same-sex marriage is a constitutional right for Colombians.

But international human-rights law was not much help to the Colombians. The lack of a bold decision on marriage equality from international human-rights bodies continues to be a problem. The European approach is even worse. States feel secure in only having to provide for civil partnerships, enshrining the difference that countries like Colombia, the US, South Africa, and Canada have rejected. It is time that international human-rights law recognises the right of queer people to marry. The battle is still to be won.

When I was writing this chapter, I was back in Japan. Now separated from G, I was there with my new girlfriend. We were in that early stage of a relationship, where your bodies and hands involuntarily move towards one another. A part of your body always wants to be touching, even if it's only the little finger. I felt shy about public affection in Japan, you don't really see it. You certainly don't see it between queer couples.

My girlfriend and I discussed going to lesbian bars in Tokyo. How hidden they are. On the third floor of an apartment block, door to the right of a lift, small bars, only for people in the know. Before smartphones, you followed the signs on lamp-posts pointing you in the direction of the bar in Shinjuku. They seem more like a friend's living room than a bar. I told my girlfriend that I went to lesbian bars in Japan when I was 25, when I had a Japanese girlfriend.

Chihiro told me then that there was no gay marriage and that gay and lesbian couples found it difficult to rent apartments. Many people, including my then girlfriend, kept their sexualities and their relationships a secret. She told me that she would definitely marry a man and have children. I even met a lesbian and gay man who were married together to avoid suspicion about their sexualities. They were open about it to me, but these secrets were only shared in queer circles. In the workplace, they were absolutely closeted.

Nearly 15 years later, I wondered how much things had changed. If anyone would think my girlfriend and I were a couple. My father didn't ask; our friends didn't either. We didn't hold hands in front of them, but I wondered if people could tell from the way we talked to one another or the way that I looked at her. 'Would you ever consider moving to Tokyo?' I asked her. 'I'm not sure,' she said. It was far away from home in Europe, but also we might be forced back into a more closeted life. Don't ask, don't tell. It would be difficult to be a couple in that situation. To have children. To try and live openly, with pride.

A few days after we flew back to Spain, the Sapporo High Court, a court in the north of Japan, ruled that denying same-sex marriage is unconstitutional on the basis that it violates the right to equality and the right to marry. It was the sixth court decision in Japan to hold that the lack of marriage equality violates the Japanese constitution. The decision has been appealed to the Supreme Court. If the Supreme Court upholds the decision, Japan could join Nepal, Taiwan, and Thailand as countries that provide marriage equality in Asia, a continent where much remains to be done for LGBTQ+ rights.

I read the news back home in Madrid with delight. 'Hey, look,' I said to my girlfriend, who was busy cutting up baby cucumbers in her kitchen. 'It looks like Japan might bring in gay marriage. Who knows when exactly, but a case is going to the Supreme Court. Maybe we could get married there next time,' I joked. She smiled, non-committal, and told me to pour her a glass of wine.

Chapter 6
You're Having My Baby

Every person and every couple I know who has a child has been on their own journey to start a family, regardless of their sexuality. But being queer and trying to have a kid is complicated. Within queer communities, there is a spectrum of complication, with gay men and trans folks facing bigger challenges than lesbian couples. Yet queer families not only exist, but are growing and thriving.

Of course, there are many queers who have no interest in reproduction or (re)producing 'heteronormative' models of the family. Queer people have long created our own families, comprising important lifelong kinship structures that sit outside of legal regulation. My friend Spruce who's from Liverpool has queer Texan aunts that she met over the internet. The iconic documentary *Paris Is Burning* shows the drag houses that make up the homes of drag queens and trans women in New York who have been adopted by 'drag mothers'. Family can take on many different shapes and forms, especially as many queer people continue to be very painfully rejected by their own families.

Queer people have also created more-traditional families for generations. I know many people in their 40s who were brought up by lesbian parents. My friend Sean has said of his mums that the worst part wasn't having lesbian mums, but being brought up a vegetarian. The film *The Birdcage* depicts two dads bringing up a son. Long before marriage equality and legal parental recognition, queer people have been doing it by themselves and for themselves. Today, the law is slowly moving forward in many countries to give queer people the chance to have children on their own or as a couple.

It's not a strange question on a Tinder date for queer people to now discuss where they stand on having children. Pretty much every woman I've ever dated has told me that she wants to have kids. This can happen on a first date or the first romantic night spent together. The question now is how we do it. Adoptions? Pregnancy? IVF in a clinic or insemination at home? Co-parenting as a lesbian couple with the involvement of a gay donor? Single parenting? Surrogacy?

One way in which queer people have become parents is through the process of adoption. When I was training as a barrister, I had a girlfriend in London who wanted to adopt children. She went to speak to someone who worked in an adoption agency to find out if a lesbian woman or couple could adopt, and she was told that it was possible. In England, Wales, and Scotland back in 2013 when she was asking these questions, couples — irrespective of marital status or sexual orientation — could adopt children and provide them with a necessary home. The legislation to allow unmarried heterosexual and gay couples to adopt had come into force in 2002. I was shocked. In Northern Ireland, gay couples and unmarried heterosexual couples could not adopt. I had grown up thinking that gay people couldn't have children. I think my mother did too, which is why she was so worried when I came out.

She was right to worry. As of 2024, only 36 countries have made joint adoption by same-sex couples available, and only 37 countries have made it legal for a second parent to adopt the child of the first parent where they are in a same-sex relationship. On the African continent, only South Africa, which famously enshrines protection against discrimination on the grounds of sexual orientation, allows for same-sex adoptions. In Asia, only Israel and Taiwan allow for it. Most of the countries that allow queer people or couples to adopt are those that also provide for marriage equality.

But in the same year that my ex-girlfriend was making enquiries about adoption and sending me into a complete tailspin about whether I wanted to settle down or not, the Northern Ireland Human Rights Commission won a case concerning gay adoptions. The Court of Appeal found that the legislation banning unmarried heterosexual couples and same-sex couples from adopting was discriminatory. This meant that in 2013 the ban on gay couples adopting was removed and the law was brought into line with other parts of the UK. In my late 20s, gay couples in Northern Ireland finally gained the opportunity to apply to adopt children.

The decision by the Court of Appeal in Northern

Ireland mirrors the approach taken by the European Court of Human Rights in a case called *X v Austria* that was decided in the same year. The court found that once a state allows unmarried heterosexual couples to adopt, it can't decline to open up adoption to unmarried queer couples. This was a landmark decision for a lesbian couple who wanted the second parent to be able to adopt their son.

Two years after Northern Ireland brought in legislation to allow queer people to adopt, the Northern Irish health minister resigned after allegedly making homophobic remarks to a lesbian couple and linking gay relationships to child abuse. The problem remains that, in too many countries, queer people are seen as anathema to traditional family structures. The right-wing rhetoric that queer people and trans people are 'groomers' feeds into a dangerous narrative that undermines queer parenthood and paints us as deviant monsters to be kept away from children. Nothing could be further from the truth.

I'm a proud queer parent, and my daughter's social circle is luckily made up of other kids being raised by single queer parents or other queer couples. There is no evidence that being brought up by queer parents means that a child is more likely to grow up gay or trans. In fact, nearly every queer person I know was raised by heterosexual parents.

Damaging myths and prejudices continue to prevent queer people from being able to adopt their partner's child or adopt a child on their own or together in many legal systems. It is clearly discriminatory if a state allows unmarried heterosexual couples or single parents to adopt but then excludes someone solely on the basis of their sexual orientation or gender identity. The eligibility criteria should always centre on the best interests of the child, rather than the prejudices of a heteronormative state.

Although some queer people and couples seek to adopt, many LGBTQ+ people want to have their own biological child. This is a deeply personal decision. As reproductive technologies have developed, queer people have more options available to achieve their dream of becoming parents in different ways. To create a baby together as a part of 'the skeleton architectures of our lives', as Audre Lorde would say. Often this is an arduous process. You cannot imagine the number of times I have wished that I could make accidental babies with a partner — make love and take the risk of having a baby together. But for queer people, we must plan, hope, and really want, in the long journey to become parents.

It was proving too difficult for G to get pregnant. Through the public system, we were able to access three rounds of fertility treatment in Madrid. But that had not worked. Our next option was to seek treatment privately. We tried the ROPA method, with G trying to carry my egg, but that didn't work either. Round after round of progesterone and oestrogen injections. It was hard not to despair at times from the highs of hope to the lows of an implantation that didn't work. Finally, it seemed that the only choice left for us, other than adoption, was that I would try fertility treatment. This was not the plan.

At an academic law workshop, I ended up chatting to a friend of mine, Monica, who had gone through fertility treatment with her wife and had children. In this chance encounter in the coffee break, we chatted intensely about fertility treatments and the choices available to a lesbian couple (or a trans or non-binary person who can get pregnant). It seemed insane that in the age of the internet and with so much information online, we were still unsure about which options are open and available. Is it best to have fertility treatment in the UK? What about Denmark or Spain? What are the financial implications and the practicalities of travelling abroad for fertility treatment? Which countries allow for known donors, and which require anonymity? The fact that nearly every country has different regulations makes it a legal minefield, and that is if you can afford the treatment.

Monica told me that she had conceived her twins in a clinic in Denmark since they wanted to be able to pick the donor. They were able to see photos of him as a baby, hear his voice, know about his hobbies and personality. They were able to choose the characteristics that they wanted from a donor, much like you might do with a male partner. Monica and her wife were now trying to have another baby and had decided that they wouldn't go back to Denmark. Due to their work, it had been hard to travel, so they had decided to try a clinic close to their house in London. Having been through the process once, they weren't so concerned about the donor specifics. This time they just wanted another baby. I listened to what Monica was saying with great interest as we had been looking into our options. G had been going through the treatment in Spain, which provides for donor anonymity, but now that I was going to go through the process, I had to decide what my priorities were.

In Madrid, G could access fertility treatment in the public health system because her organisation had litigated the case to allow single women and queer women access to IVF. The law in Spain has further developed since then, making it one of the most progressive in Europe. Lesbian couples no longer need to be married to access ROPA treatment. In February 2023, the Spanish government also passed *Law 4/2023*, known colloquially as the *Trans Law*, which stipulates that trans men should have access to assisted reproduction, without discrimination. In the gender-identity unit at the healthcare centre I attend in Madrid, I have frequently been asked about my thoughts on fertility and whether I want to preserve my eggs. It is progressive and important for healthcare to be inclusive of the specific situations of LGBTQ+ people. But across Europe, there is no uniformity on access to fertility treatment.

In Italy, single women and same-sex couples do not have access to assisted-reproduction treatments. It was only in 2021 that France changed its law to allow single women and lesbian couples to access IVF treatments for the first time. Before this, French lesbians were travelling to Spain to access IVF. My friends living in Bulgaria have told me that their situation is extremely difficult. The system not only prohibits lesbians and single women from accessing IVF, but also refuses to recognise same-sex couples. While laws are constantly changing, most countries still have no IVF equality for same-sex couples, and many lesbians have to travel and pay for their treatment in order to access donor treatment.

I looked into treatment in Spain and in the UK and concluded that the only way I could get fertility treatment was by going privately. I lived in London so was not entitled to healthcare on the Spanish system, and in the UK the eligibility criteria excluded same-sex couples at the initial threshold — since a woman had to prove that she had failed to conceive after a year of unprotected vaginal intercourse. There was no way that I could meet that criteria. I spoke to lesbians I knew, and they all told me either that they had decided to get pregnant at home with a friend as the sperm donor or that they had gone to private fertility clinics in the UK or abroad. The public health system, which should be for everyone, excluded queers. This is particularly difficult for trans and lesbian couples, who tend to be less likely to have the means to pay for private services.

In 2021, a year after I had my child, social-media influencers Whitney and Megan Bacon-Evans, jointly known as Wegan, launched a test case arguing that a branch of the National Health Service (NHS) in England discriminates against LGBT families. Wegan challenged the rule that same-sex female couples, as well as single women, had to pay for 12 insemination treatments privately to prove medical infertility before they could get treatment on the NHS. The influencers were represented by lawyers including Jude Bunting KC, my old roommate in chambers, who argued in their claim that the policy was directly and indirectly discriminatory on the basis of their sexual orientation. The lawyers explained that even if the couple attempted 12 cycles of insemination at home with a private sperm donor, or attempted an insemination every day for two years at home, they would still not be eligible to meet the criteria, which required them to undergo six rounds of insemination in a clinical setting, at an estimated cost of thousands of pounds. The couple argued this breached both the *Equality Act* and the European Convention on Human Rights.

As *Women's Health* magazine has explained, the costs involved in the eligibility requirements 'created an impassable financial barrier for many queer couples and single women wanting to start a family'. The UK organisation Stonewall started a campaign with the hashtag #IVFForAll. In 2022, the government announced plans to provide access to IVF treatment to non-heterosexual couples and to single women as part of its first-ever Women's Health Strategy. *DIVA* magazine, a media source for LGBTQ+ women and non-binary people, described it as 'a huge win for IVF equality'. Despite the Women's Health Strategy coming into force in 2022, as of April 2024, only four of the NHS's 42 integrated-care bodies have made changes to their IVF policy, meaning that most LGBTQ+ people do not have access to publicly funded treatment in England. In Northern Ireland, lesbian couples still have to fund four rounds of artificial insemination before they are eligible for public funding. In 2023, Wegan withdrew their legal challenge after their local health service agreed to change its fertility treatment rules for lesbian couples.

The situation is even more complicated for cis gay men, who cannot get pregnant. Gay men in the UK and

New York have launched legal challenges claiming that their exclusion from IVF funding or eligibility is discriminatory. In March 2024, a gay couple in New York filed a class-action suit stating that the city's health-insurance plan was discriminatory because the only group excluded from IVF funding eligibility are men or male couples. The couple are seeking insurance to cover the costs of IVF to create an embryo, which they could then implant in a surrogate. The couple complain that gay men cannot meet the infertility criteria for IVF and that the criteria only enables women, or men with female partners, to be eligible for IVF benefits. According to news reports, the two men have said they expect to pay $100,000 for the IVF costs and an additional $165,000 for surrogacy. The case is ongoing. A similar case is pending in Northern Ireland, where two men are seeking public funding for IVF treatment. They had an agreement with a surrogate in Northern Ireland but sought public funding for egg donation. Their case was rejected in the High Court and has moved to the Court of Appeal.

Obtaining the right to access fertility treatment and funding in a clinical setting is just one battle for LGBTQ+ parents and rainbow families. There is a separate and related fight to allow us to conceive where and when we want and with whom we want. In many countries, the law does not make this possible. In fact, in most countries in Europe, home insemination — that is, the insertion of sperm — is prohibited, and there is a risk that one of the lesbian parents will not be recognised as such if insemination occurs outside of a clinical setting.

The situation in the UK is different. In England and Wales, if two women are married and get pregnant via fertility treatment in a registered clinic or conceive through DIY artificial insemination at home, the couple will both be on the birth certificate and be recognised as the legal parents. But there is an important exception to a lesbian married couple both being recognised as the legal parents. Remember that terrible Spike Lee film *She Hate Me* (2004)? In it, tons of hot lesbians pay a former business executive $10,000 to have sex with them so that they become pregnant. The film depicts many of the lesbians enjoying the sexual intercourse and getting pregnant. This is terrible not only for centring the male fantasy of lesbians as women who really harbour a secret desire to have sex with men, but also for putting lesbians at legal risk. In many jurisdictions, including the UK, having sex with a man gives him parental rights if the woman gets pregnant and has a baby. The pregnant woman's partner would not be recognised as a legal parent. So be warned that the law makes a distinction based on how conception takes place. Hence the importance of the turkey baster.

The UK is one of the rare places in Europe where married lesbians have a choice: at a clinic or at home, with a known or unknown donor (but the law changes all the time, so make sure you get legal advice before embarking on this). This raises the question of the practicalities. How do you do the insemination at home? I googled this while I was going through the first round of the medicalised process to donate my eggs to G. Oestradiol, progesterone, and a general anaesthetic for the medical treatment were taking their toll on me. The hormones were making me depressed, bloated, and irritated. I wasn't sure to be honest if it was the hormones or the fact that I was living a near-monastic life. I had stopped drinking and was eating lots of vegetables that were orange in colour. I was getting weekly acupuncture. I was trying to do yoga and exercise mildly but not excessively. It was July, Spanish summer, and all my friends were having fun, drinking Aperol spritz, and calling me about their latest escapades. While I had entered the horrendous vortex of medically assisted reproduction. I started googling because I was sick of it all and desperate for the process to end. I thought there must be a less medically invasive way to do this, to get pregnant.

What I learnt online was that that DIY insemination isn't so complicated. There are numerous articles and video clips on YouTube that explain how to go about it, while expressing a caveat to seek medical advice. Queer people who can get pregnant (lesbians, trans dudes, non-binary folks) were recording their temperature every day and making a basal body chart, which can help predict the exact day of ovulation. There are even apps to help you track period dates and identify the ideal dates for conception. Is this what straight people do, I wondered?

Once the dates are identified, then it's just about inserting the sperm. This is where the internet really comes into its own. Soon I saw mentions of the term 'Mosie Baby'. I had no idea what that was, so I googled further. I didn't need to look much, because Wegan have a dedicated video on home insemination. The social-media femmes open up their package of Mosie Baby, which it turns out is a 'stunning' turkey baster shaped as a tampon to help get sperm to the uterus. The influencers then announce a giveaway to femmes who are looking for femmes. I closed the video. I felt sick from the pink and product placement.

Whatever my views on unboxing videos for the Mosie Baby, laws banning home insemination have a real impact on queer people trying to get pregnant. Waiting lists in public clinics are often extremely long, and access to private fertility treatment is expensive and prohibitive for most people. At-home insemination is also currently only available in the UK for those who are married, and many queer women don't want to enter into marriages. In most countries, unmarried queer women must have treatment in a registered clinic for both to be recognised automatically on the birth certificate.

We must have a wider conversation on the benefits and risks of home insemination, with the UK model being one that provides queer people from all socio-economic backgrounds with an opportunity to get pregnant and also to establish their own kinship structures outside of the medicalised process. As a queer person, I want to have the right to choose a donor, to try to get pregnant in my own home, to decide whether to do so in a fertility clinic or not, to have the treatment covered by the state, and to understand my legal protections. I believe that this forms part of our right to bodily autonomy. To choose and control the way in which we get pregnant. As it stands for too many queer people, almost everywhere in the world, parenthood is expensive and complex.

When my daughter was just about to turn three years old, we were flying home from a holiday together. She was so excited about being on an aeroplane. She is friendly and very chatty. She sat in the middle seat and struck up a conversation with an older woman beside her. The woman talked about their names and said her own name was G—.

'That's my mum's name,' said my daughter proudly.

'Oh,' the woman said, turning to me, 'you are G— as well.'

'No,' I said, 'I'm called Keio.'

'I have two mums,' my toddler said with even more pride (this was during my transition, but that's a story for another day).

'That's not possible,' the woman said, 'there's no one like Mum and there's only one mother!'

My daughter looked at me, then at the woman, and said, 'I have two mums.'

The woman looked at me, giving me a look that said *silly two-year-old*.

'She has two mothers,' I explained patiently to the woman. 'Some people have one mother, some people have two. Some people have a dad, some people have two.'

The woman stopped talking to us after that. Maybe she was embarrassed; maybe she was a bigot. I didn't even want to get into the whole *I'm one of the legal mothers, but I'm trans* topic. Sitting in row 8F, I think we had all had enough for the day, and I certainly didn't want my daughter to be exposed to any potential toxicity.

Either way, the conversation raised something that the courts are now dealing with — who gets to be mother? And why can there only be one? My daughter's response to the woman on the plane is one that all judges should have to listen to. You can have two mothers, you can have two fathers, you can have one mother, or one father, or you can have a mother who becomes a father, and all can be wonderful parents who love their children, and children know that's what matters.

In many legal systems, the law simply won't recognise that a child has two mothers or two fathers. For example, in Italy, where IVF and fertility treatment is banned for single women and lesbians, lesbian families have been going abroad to have their children. They obtain birth certificates in countries like Spain that recognise shared motherhood and then return to Italy to raise the child. But that is when new problems can start. In 2023, 33 lesbian families in Padua found themselves in a legal battle after government officials challenged the children's birth certificates on the grounds that it was illegal for a child to have two mothers. The officials requested the removal of the non-gestational mother from the birth certificates. The situation is extremely painful, not only for the mothers, but also for their wider families and the children, with court cases likely to drag out over years.

This is absolute cruelty leading to the forced migration and expulsion of queer people who have to choose between staying in a country that is their home in order to have their right to family life recognised or going somewhere they have more protection. It is heartbreaking for the children, who could suddenly have one of their mothers removed from their documents. Clearly such decisions are not in the best interests of a child. Yet, many countries around the world simply won't recognise LGBTQ+ parents as co-parents in law or will even take steps to try to remove a parent.

The failure to recognise rainbow families has many significant and practical impacts on queer families and children, including in relation to immigration, residence, and citizenship rights. In 2022, *The Guardian* published an article on how children born outside the UK to British parents in same-sex relationships are being left 'stateless'. The article described the nightmare situation and landmark legal challenge of a lesbian couple who were not able to obtain a passport for their child. Jane, one of the mothers, was born in Gibraltar but has British citizenship by descent. Her partner is Bulgarian, and they have a daughter, Sara, who was born in Spain. But when Sara was born, she was left stateless. The UK Home Office said that Sara is not entitled to British citizenship because both she and her mum were born outside of the UK. Bulgaria refused to issue her with a passport, saying that they don't recognise non-conventional families. Sara also cannot acquire Spanish citizenship, because neither of her parents are Spanish. The couple had little choice but to litigate their case to the Court of Justice of the European Union (CJEU), the court that decides cases on matters of EU law.

On 9 February 2021, the CJEU heard how Bulgaria had rejected Sara's citizenship application on the basis that a baby cannot have two mothers. The CJEU responded, as it often has done, by handing down a positive judgment for LGBTQ+

parents. It ruled that Bulgaria must issue Sara with identity documents so that the family can exercise their right to free movement in the EU. The court was also clear that once an EU member state issues a birth certificate, other member states have to recognise it. In 2024, I spoke to the family's lawyer and asked if Sara had received her travel documents. Sara is four and a half years old, just months older than my child, and she has still not been issued with travel documents or been able to go to Bulgaria to see her family.

Travelling with my kid on the aeroplane, I thought of Sara and how much I take our freedom of movement for granted. To visit family and friends, to go on holiday with my three-year-old. An estimated two million children currently face a situation in which a recognition of their parenthood in one EU country is not recognised in another EU country. A new proposed law within the EU seeks to recognise parenthood 'irrespective of how the child was conceived or born and irrespective of the type of family of the child'. The law would create an EU parenthood certificate so that LGBTQ+ parents and their child have a document confirming their family relationship in situations where national authorities refuse to do so. These documents are fundamental so that families can move and reside freely together.

A common identity document would be particularly beneficial for couples who have children via surrogacy outside of the EU. Many couples in Europe struggle with government regulations that ban commercial surrogacy arrangements or make it difficult for the parents to be recognised as such in their own countries. I didn't know much about surrogacy, so I decided to call my friend Lucille and ask her about her motherhood journey.

Lucille, a single queer woman, had her baby via a surrogate in the US. She explained that those who have their babies that way are called 'intended parents' and find their surrogates through regulated agencies in states such as California. The agency fees, surrogacy expenses, fertility treatment, and paying for lawyers all totalled around $200,000 once she also factored in travel. The surrogate gave birth to her child, Lucille's genetic child, meaning that the embryo was created with her eggs and sperm from a donor. The surrogate has no genetic link to the child. Lucille maintains a close relationship with her surrogate, sharing photos of her son. I was shocked to learn that her surrogate was a middle-class married woman with her own career. Lucille explained that her surrogate had wanted to do it after having her own children. She lives in her own house in the suburbs of California, a far cry from media reports about baby farms and surrogacy dorms in countries such as India and Nepal.

In 2018, Olympic diver Tom Daley and his husband, Dustin Lance Black, made national headlines after announcing the birth of their child via a surrogate. Black, a Hollywood filmmaker, has explained that in the US their news was met with congratulations, while in the UK reactions were mixed. Journalist Richard Littlejohn wrote a column in the *Daily Mail* with the title 'Please don't pretend two dads is the new normal'. Black went on to make a podcast series for

BBC Radio called *Surrogacy: A Family Frontier*, detailing their journey to build their family. While Black might have been surprised that the reactions were different in the US and UK, it does not surprise me. In the UK, and even more so in Europe, the legal regulations around commercial surrogacy reflect a discomfort with the practice.

In England and Wales, surrogacy is legal. But surrogacy agreements cannot be enforced by the law. It is a criminal offence to advertise that you are looking for a surrogate or willing to act as a surrogate. It is also a criminal offence for a solicitor or lawyer to negotiate the terms of a surrogacy agreement for payment. So while surrogacy is legal, there are a number of criminal laws that make the surrogacy process in the UK far from straightforward. Surrogacy in the UK therefore has to take place via an altruistic arrangement and on the basis of trust. Under these arrangements, surrogates can be paid their reasonable expenses. When surrogacy agreements break down, they can result in messy and complicated litigation in the family courts to determine who the child will live with and who gets the right to make parental decisions about the child.

In England, to have a child via a surrogate, you must be genetically related to the child. If a child is born via surrogacy, the surrogate and her spouse will be registered as the mother and father, and the intended parents will have to apply for a parental order. If the surrogate isn't married, then the biological intended parent, usually the person who provided sperm, can be registered as the father or second parent. As Lady Hale explained in the case *Whittington Hospital NHS Trust v XX*, 'the surrogate mother is always the child's legal parent unless and until a court order is made in favour of the commissioning parents'. Intended parents therefore require a parental order. This is all very different to California, where the intended parents automatically go on the birth certificate. My friend Lucille is listed as the sole parent of her child. The birth certificate gave her a choice whether to register as the mother, father, or parent of the child. She chose the mother option.

Some years ago, two gay dads challenged the law in the UK as they wanted to be put on the birth certificate after they had a child with a surrogate. The national courts and then the European Court of Human Rights (in *H v United Kingdom*) all found that the UK could specify that the surrogate was the mother, and that the person who gives birth has to go on the birth certificate. They also accepted that the birth certificate could register the surrogate's husband on the birth certificate, even if he is not the biological father. The rationale for this is 'the potential for considerable uncertainty regarding the parentage of a child born by way of assisted reproduction'. Which does absolutely nothing to explain why the surrogate's husband is listed on the birth certificate as the father when it is known that he is not in fact the biological father at all. Meanwhile, the ECHR 'has not held that the intended parents must immediately and automatically be recognised as such in law'. The court decided that the biological father did not need to be on the birth certificate and that there was no breach of his human rights since the intended parents could obtain parental orders confirming their parentage.

The laws in the UK may soon change. In 2023, the Law Commission of England and Wales recommended a new system to simplify the process and allow intended parents to become the legal parents of the child from birth, though this would be subject to the surrogate's right to withdraw her consent. The Law Commission noted that currently some couples have to wait up to a year after birth before they become the legal parents of their child.

Some countries in Europe, such as Italy, are moving in the opposite direction and making it illegal for families to travel abroad and have babies via commercial surrogacy arrangements. Countries such as France have refused to grant parental recognition to intended parents, even where there is, for example, a US birth certificate confirming that they are the parents of the child and the child is theirs biologically. According to a 2019 study conducted in 43 European countries, surrogacy is prohibited in 24 of those countries, tolerated in ten, and permitted in nine. The arguments given for prohibition or restriction include:

- that surrogacy creates a risk of the exploitation of vulnerable women
- that surrogacy for payment is a form of trafficking and makes children vulnerable to sale
- that it is important to discourage commercial surrogacy arrangements to protect children from being turned into a commodity
- that surrogacy is against public order.

These arguments have been used by governments not only to restrict surrogacy domestically, but also in court proceedings to deny legal parent-child recognition. As more families have turned to surrogacy to grow their families, the ECHR has increasingly been called upon to decide cases on this issue. Summarising the position of the court remains far from straightforward, but in a nutshell, through a number of cases, the court has established that a country cannot create an absolute prohibition against recognising a biological child born to a surrogate, while countries can refuse to recognise such relationships or even remove children from the care of intended parents where there is no biological link.

One of the early cases, *Mennesson v France*, demonstrates the legal quagmire that parents face in European countries when they have children via surrogacy abroad. A married heterosexual couple decided to go to the United States to have a child via a surrogacy agreement after they found out that the wife was infertile. The couple underwent IVF and created embryos with the husband's sperm and entered into a gestational surrogacy agreement. According to the court documents, the surrogate was not remunerated and only received reimbursement for expenses, and both she and her husband were high earners, with a much greater income than the French couple. She told the couple that she wanted to do it as 'an act of solidarity'. The surrogate became pregnant with twins, who were born on 25 October 2000. When the twins were born, the couple were issued with two birth certificates stating that they were the parents.

Following the birth of the children in Los Angeles, the parents attended to register the birth certificate at the French consulate. However, the consulate refused to register them or give them French travel documents, and instead decided to refer them to the public prosecutor's office in France.

The family travelled back to France using the children's American passports. The couple were placed under criminal investigation, and four years after the birth of the children, a judge finally dismissed the case against the couple, finding that no crime had been committed, since having a child abroad was not a punishable offence in France.

Meanwhile, the parents continued to try and record the birth of their children in the French national register. As of 2014, when the parents brought the case to the ECHR, the French authorities had still to issue certificates of French nationality for the now 14-year-old children. The parents complained to the ECHR that, to the detriment of their family rights, they were unable to obtain recognition in France of the legal parent-child relationship and that this violated their right to private and family life under the European Convention on Human Rights.

The court noted in its judgment that surrogacy arrangements raise sensitive ethical issues and that regulations between states greatly vary. It heard arguments from France that French law considers surrogacy agreements to be 'null and void' and that it would be against public policy to register the children. The French government argued that if they registered the children, it would be tacitly accepting a situation in which parents had circumvented French law to have children. The court noted the practical difficulties that the twins faced when being enrolled at school, at the canteen, at an outdoor centre, and in social security. They were unable to obtain French nationality. The parents explained that this complicated travel as a family and raised concerns at border control as to why the parents are French and the children are American. The parents also worried about what would happen to the residence status of the children once they were over the age of 18.

Despite these difficulties, the court held that the human rights of the parents had not been breached. The parents had been able to bring the twins back to France and live as a family in the country. However, the court found that the right to private and family life of the children had been violated. It explained that the right to private life requires that everyone should be able to establish details of their identity as individual human beings, including details of the legal parent-child relationship, and that 'an essential aspect of the identity of individuals is at stake where the legal parent-child relationship is concerned'. The court found that the children were recognised in US law but not in French law and that a 'contradiction of that nature undermines the children's identity within French society'. It held that the refusal to recognise the parent-child relationship in French law impacted a range of identity rights of the children, including their nationality, inheritance, and best interests.

In this case and in case law since, the ECHR has determined that countries must provide some form of recognition of childred born abroad via surrogacy where there is a biological connection between the children and the intended father. Where there are two intended fathers, a country must provide the second father with an opportunity to adopt the child. This is important for the rights of the child and to ensure that there is legal equality between the parents.

The court has taken a very different view when it comes to intended mothers. In the case of *D v France*, a heterosexual couple had a child via a surrogacy arrangement in Ukraine. They created an embryo from the husband's sperm and the wife's egg, and the baby was carried by a surrogate. But France refused to record in the French register of births, marriages, and deaths the details of the birth certificate of the child insofar as the certificate designated the intended mother — also the biological mother — as the mother. The husband was registered as the father, however. The ECHR found that there was no violation of human rights in this because the intended mother could go through an adoption procedure, and held that a biological mother's rights are not violated under the European Convention on Human Rights if she has to adopt her own child. The court gave France a wider 'margin of appreciation' to determine who it designates as mother on the birth certificate, deploying a hands-off approach.

This is hard to square with the court's own analysis when it comes to intended, biological fathers. In *Mennesson v France*, it made clear that:

> Having regard to the importance of biological parentage as a component of identity ... it cannot be said to be in the interests of the child to deprive him or her of a legal relationship of this nature where the biological reality of that relationship has been established and the child and parent concerned demand full recognition thereof.

There are important conversations that we need to continue to have to ensure that the different human rights of all those involved in surrogacy arrangements are protected: this includes the rights of surrogates, intended parents, and children born from surrogacy agreements.

The approach of the European Court of Human Rights is that a child has a right to know its biological parentage and that states must take into account the best interests of the child to have the legal parent relationship recognised. But as we have seen from the cases above, the court picks and chooses whose biology. In *D v France*, why is the father 'father' because he provided sperm when a mother is not recognised in law as mother when she provides her egg? Is 'mother' always the woman who gives birth? Is 'mother' only the woman who gives birth? Or is the reality that there can be more than one mother? Or in the case of D, is the wife the mother and the surrogate a surrogate? To me, it is clear that my friend Lucille is the mother of her child. Just as in lesbian couples, both women can be mothers.

One of the major problems I have with the current approach is the gendered differentiation and hierarchy of biological matter. I wonder if this could all be fixed if we could simply have the word 'parent' on a birth certificate? What would it mean to degender our parenting roles? Would it really be so scary?

After we got married and G and I had a child, G told her father, a former judge in Spain, that she had had a baby. Her father asked her a series of questions, including who had given birth to our child. G told him I had given birth to the child.

There was silence on the phone. He told her that he did not recognise our daughter as his grandchild. He rejected her. He rejected us. His comment was devastating for G and infuriated me.

Despite advancements in the law in countries such as Spain, which was one of the first countries in the world to legislate for gay marriage, cultural prejudice remains entrenched. Many people continue to see gay relationships as less than heterosexual ones. As abnormal. A type of relationship to remain in the shadows rather than to be celebrated.

His reaction to the news was his loss. The news of our child's birth was a cause for celebration with our family and friends in the dark days of the pandemic. But the rejection served as a reminder to me that legal change is not the end of the road. We have to continue to tell stories, to have the conversations that my friends were having as they canvassed on doorsteps in Los Angeles and Dublin. The battle to turn hearts and minds away from prejudice and towards pride continues. And the battle for queer family rights, including rights to our own children, remains one of the most urgent challenges that we face today.

Chapter 7
Born This Way

I had huge reservations about pregnancy. While many straight women fear the changes it will provoke in their bodies, I worried about what it would do to my sense of gender. How could I keep hold of my masculinity and genderqueer identity if I was pregnant? How was it that I was now contemplating something traditionally associated with womanhood when I felt myself so far from that identification? How would I manage? Seeking comfort, I found inspiration in the stories of trans men giving birth. I also laughed along with the graphic novel *Pregnant Butch*, based on the author A.K. Summers's experience of pregnancy as 'nine long months spent in drag'.

Could I manage nine months in drag? I would soon find out. After two rounds of treatment, I took a pregnancy test. I couldn't believe what I saw: two clear red lines. After four years of trying and multiple rounds of fertility treatment, we finally had a positive result.

This was in early 2020. In a matter of weeks after finding out that I was pregnant, the world shut down. The Covid-19 pandemic locked me in my house. My meetings, court hearings, and social life were all mediated through a screen.

For many of us who became parents during the pandemic, pregnancy was scary. Appointments were solitary. Partners couldn't attend scans, or sometimes even the birth. Some pregnant women with Covid died. Even after the vaccine rollout, there were so many unknowns. Pregnant people and their partners were worried about how the pandemic would affect their pregnancies and impact their choices when giving birth. The one solace was that my pregnant body was invisible to all but the handful of family members and close friends that I saw in those nine months when lockdown restrictions eased.

In 2020, I gave birth to my child in the same hospital where I was born.

There are two questions people ask when you have a baby: 'What's the name?' and 'Is it a boy or a girl?' From the moment a child is born (sometimes even beforehand, as shown by the trend of gender-reveal parties), gender becomes a social marker that impacts how a child is raised and treated in society. Boys don't cry. Girls must smile and be polite. Boys will be boys. And so it goes. We received gifts for our new baby, sent in the mail because we couldn't see anybody. Sometimes these were cuddly toys and neutral-coloured growsuits. But many friends and family members couldn't help themselves from sending bundles of pink clothing.

Some days after the birth, I went to register my child's name in the town council. We were back in a lockdown and London was deserted. The registrar was a wonderful, bubbly woman from South London. She congratulated me on the birth of our child and said that the baby was so lucky to have two mums. Then she explained the rules on who was mum and who was parent. I was stunned. I hadn't thought about this. She explained that in England and Wales, the mother is the person who gives birth. The other mother — in this case, G — would be registered on the birth certificate as 'parent'. One mother, one parent. Exhausted, still sore from giving birth, and sleep-deprived, I finished the paperwork and left with my child's birth certificate. It was the inverse of how we wanted to be labelled: the genderqueer person, me, ending up as 'mother' and G designated as 'parent'. It was only later that I learnt that 'parent' is not a gender-neutral term in English law: it is the designation for the female parent who does not give birth, i.e. the other mother.

Then after four months in London, we decided to move to Spain. It took us four more months to complete the paperwork to register our child for her Spanish citizenship and documents. Even though she had a UK birth certificate, she would also get a Spanish birth certificate through G, who is Spanish. In Spain, they have what is called a family book. To obtain this document, first we had to register our marriage and the birth with a judge. We sat before her in a municipal office in Madrid and she explained how our child would be registered in Spain.

'So,' the judge said to me, 'you are going to be Mother B because your surname is the second surname, and G, you are Mother A because your surname is the child's first surname.' I had to stifle a laugh. In Spain, we could both be mother. In the UK, only one mother is allowed. The law in Spain gives lesbian couples what they want and reflects their realities as co-mothers in the process. It also does not distinguish motherhood based on who has gestated the baby. But it didn't give me the option of being parent and G being mother.

It was only by going through pregnancy and birth registration that I truly grasped how the law regulates queer bodies that reproduce. How the law operates as a fiction denying us our authentic lived realities. It sees intersex, genderqueer, and trans people as scary monsters, and tries to mould our queer lives into the binary. Trans men, non-binary people, and intersex people get pregnant — that's our reality. As a barrister, I can't see any reason why the baby's birth certificate can't register G as the mother and me the gestational parent or birth parent. There is no displacement of women's rights in this situation. It simply extends and amplifies rights to reflect rainbow families, including mothers like G who have not gestated. But birth certificates fail to recognise this gendered spectrum within parenthood.

A week after registering my child's birth, I read a piece in *The Guardian* headlined 'Trans man loses UK legal battle to register as his child's father'. Freddy McConnell, a 34-year-old journalist, had given birth and wanted to appear on the child's birth certificate as 'father', 'parent', or even 'gestational parent'. Instead, he was told he would have to be registered as 'mother', which he argued breached the *Human Rights Act 1998*. Even in my post-birth haze I read the piece with great interest. McConnell and I were the same age. He had taken a step that I wanted to explore, and his situation was a manifestation of the problems that non-binary and trans men have when they have children. I paid attention.

McConnell had been taking testosterone and had top surgery back in 2014. He had obtained a Gender Recognition Certificate (GRC), which states that 'the person to whom this certificate has been issued is for all purposes the gender shown'. His name and gender had been changed on his passport and also on his NHS documents long before that. With the GRC, his gender was also changed on his own birth certificate. In other words, the law recognises what Freddy McConnell is: a man. But what happens when a trans man gives birth? McConnell has described how he was treated with respect as a man throughout the process of becoming pregnant; it was only after he gave birth that he had to mount a challenge to be recognised as the father of his child. The High Court and the Court of Appeal rejected his legal challenge to being designated as mother, and the Supreme Court refused to hear his case. So why were the courts refusing to register a trans man, recognised in law as such, as the father or gestational parent? What about the rights of birthing dads?

Before we look at how the courts reached their decision, it's important to understand how we got to this point.

'Trans' is an umbrella term and not a homogonous concept. Sometimes non-binary identities are included within this spectrum, but trans and non-binary identities can be very different. Some trans people want to go from A to B and never to go back to A. They feel strongly that they should not be referred to by their previous name, a practice referred to sometimes as 'deadnaming', and they want surgery to live in their true gender. Jack Halberstam, a queer scholar, introduced 'trans*' to denote the fluidity and multitudes contained within the category trans. Some people who are referred to as trans do not use this word for themselves. The American writer and poet Maggie Nelson has explained in *The Argonauts* that her partner, Harry Dodge, does not use it. As Dodge explains: 'I am not on my way anywhere.' Finn Mackay, a British gender scholar, puts it like this:

> The word 'trans' means to cross, as in words like 'transport', or 'transnational'. Thus, to trans gender would mean to cross the socially constructed lines of gender, or to cross identify with a gender that one originally did not or was not able to. That is not my story.

We should all be able to use the terms and identities that best fit the way we feel about our genders. The words and terms that we use to describe genders will undoubtedly change much in the same way that the vocabulary in relation to sexuality has shifted over time as gay rights have become more established. It is part of our right to free speech and expression to be able to identify ourselves and talk in our own terms about our bodies, our sexuality, and our gender(s).

Many countries in Europe, including the UK, have refused to provide trans people with birth certificates and new identity documents, even when the public health system is providing gender-affirming care. I recently read the autobiography of Michael Dillon, a trans man who started taking testosterone in the 1930s and obtained gender-affirming surgery in the 1940s. Trans people have had gender-affirming procedures since the 1940s and 1950s but without official recognition of their genders. This led to trans people challenging the refusals to change their identity documentation before the European Court of Human Rights. The ECHR has played an important role in securing trans rights in Europe. Since 1992, it has found that countries like the UK and France have violated the rights of post-operative trans people when the authorities refused to amend a civil register or provide the trans people with new identity documents.

It was Christine Goodwin, a trans women in the UK who requested a new National Insurance number, who ended up changing the law. Goodwin's documents stated that she was male, which was causing her problems at work. She told the ECHR how she was sexually harassed by colleagues and had tried to bring a sexual-harassment claim, only to have it rejected on the basis that she was a man in the eyes of the law. She was fired from her job without protections. She wanted documentation in her female gender so that no one would know about her transition. Goodwin told the court that she had been robbed one day and hadn't felt able to report it to the police, for fear that the investigation would require her to reveal her gender identity. The lack of documentation was having a real impact on her life.

In 2002, the ECHR found that the law in the UK violated Goodwin's rights. This was significant since in a series of cases before it in the 1990s the court had decided that the UK government did not have to alter the register of births or issue new birth certificates to trans people and that their rights were not being violated. In a short space of time, the court had changed its approach to trans cases; its thinking had evolved, and the court explained that it had developed a growing consciousness of the serious problem facing 'transsexuals', including 'the stress and alienation arising from a discordance between the position in society assumed by a post-operative transsexual and the status imposed by law which refuses to recognise the change of gender'. The court explained that the law's refusal to recognise a person's social reality leads to trans people having feelings of vulnerability, humiliation, and anxiety.

Goodwin v United Kingdom established that where a state has authorised treatment and surgery, it is illogical for the state to refuse to recognise the legal implications of the result to which the treatment leads. In language that now sounds rather antiquated, the court explained that the law in the UK created an 'unsatisfactory situation in which post-operative transsexuals live in an intermediate zone as not quite one gender or the other'. It found a violation of Goodwin's rights.

Importantly, the court explained that 'society may reasonably be expected to tolerate a certain inconvenience to enable individuals to live in dignity and worth in accordance with the sexual identity chosen by them at great personal cost.' The decision led to the enactment of the *Gender Recognition Act 2004*. The Act means that trans people in the UK can change their documents, including their birth certificate, by obtaining a GRC.

Only trans men and women over the age of 18 can seek a GRC, and they must prove that they have lived full-time in their 'acquired gender' for two years before obtaining one. This proof includes documents such as driving licences, passports, and bank statements. When the government carried out a consultation on the GRC, many trans people explained that this requirement was 'humiliating and dehumanising' and that it was difficult to obtain the necessary documentation. It is not possible in the UK for people to self-identify with respect to their gender; it is an arduous process. It is also not possible to obtain a certificate with a non-binary status. The national courts have dismissed challenges to legislation that would allow people to be issued documents such as passports with a non-binary or X marker — as is allowed in Argentina, Denmark, Australia, and a growing number of countries around the world.

Trans people in the UK also have to undergo medical evaluations and obtain two medical reports that include evidence of a medical diagnosis of gender dysphoria and the details of any treatment received. One of these reports must be made by a medical practitioner specialised in gender dysphoria, which is defined by the NHS as 'a sense of unease that a person may have because of a mismatch between their biological sex and their gender identity'. The NHS website makes it clear that gender dysphoria is not a mental illness. It is also important to note that surgery or hormone treatment is not a requirement for those seeking a GRC.

You must, however, make a statutory declaration stating that you will continue to live in your new gender permanently. You must state that you are going from A to B and never want to go back to A. If you are married or in a civil partnership, you need a statutory declaration — written permission — from your spouse to transition. This is sometimes referred to as the spousal veto clause. Prior to the enactment of the *Marriage (Same Sex Couples) Act 2013*, a trans person could not obtain a GRC while being married. You had to divorce. Nowadays, if your spouse does not consent to the transition, you can apply for what's called an interim GRC while you obtain a divorce.

Once you have gathered together all of the required documents, your application goes before the Gender Recognition Panel, which decides whether or not to grant the Gender Recognition Certificate. A panel of strangers decide what your gender is. In the years 2020–2021, 466 people applied for a GRC. According to government statistics, 95 per cent of these applications were successful. Yet it is clear that obtaining a GRC is a difficult process and desperately in need of reform. I for one have not wanted to go through the medicalised process in order to obtain a GRC.

Freddy McConnell had already gone through this process, meaning that his birth certificate states that his sex is male. In 2016, he suspended taking testosterone and decided that he wanted to become a father. He had fertility treatment. Records from the fertility clinic where he accessed treatment show that his gender was registered as male. In April 2017, he became pregnant, and in January 2018 he gave birth to a son. After he gave birth, McConnell had to register the birth, but was told by the Registry Office that he had to be registered as the child's mother. He decided to challenge the decision by way of judicial review — which is a legal action challenging a government decision. McConnell was heard in the High Court, but the judge rejected his claim on the following basis:

> a) At common law a person whose egg is inseminated in their womb and who then becomes pregnant and gives birth to a child is that child's 'mother';
> b) The status of being a 'mother' arises from the role that a person has undertaken in the biological process of conception, pregnancy and birth;
> c) Being a 'mother' or a 'father' with respect to the conception, pregnancy and birth of a child is not necessarily gender specific, although until recent decades it invariably was so. It is now possible, and recognised by the law, for a 'mother' to have an acquired gender of male, and for a 'father' to have acquired gender of female ...

Even though McConnell is a man, the judge found that he could not be a 'father' in the eyes of the law because parliament had made an exception in relation to parenthood — being a mother or father was not affected by the *Gender Recognition Act*. The court found that Section 12 of the Act has a specific provision on parenthood: 'The fact that a person's gender has become the acquired gender under this Act does not affect the status of the person as the father or mother of a child.'

On the question of who is mother, the judge had this to say:

> It is undoubtedly the case that throughout history the role of being a gestational mother has been undertaken by females, but is being female the essential or determining attribute of motherhood? There is a strong case to be made for the role of 'mother' being ascribed to the person, irrespective of gender, who undertakes the carrying of a pregnancy and who gives birth to a child. In that regard, being a 'mother' is to describe a person's role in the biological process of conception, pregnancy and birth; no matter what else a mother may do, this role is surely at the essence of what a 'mother' undertakes with respect to a child to whom they give birth. It is a matter of the role taken in the biological process, rather the person's particular sex or gender.

The judge concluded that the 'concept of a male mother is therefore not unknown to the law'. While dismissing McConnell's case, the High Court did understand the importance of the case. The judge explained that 'Down the centuries, no court has previously been required to determine the definition of "mother" under English common law and, it seems, that there have been few comparable decisions made in other courts elsewhere in the Western World.' Essentially, the judge held that there was a pressing need for parliament to look at this area of law.

I was upset with the judgment. Mostly for men like Freddy McConnell who have already gone through the GRC process, but also for myself. After my pregnancy, I was sure that I never wanted to have a child again as a woman, but that I would consider it as a birthing dad. But either way, in the UK, the law would designate me as mother if I gave birth. I found the reasoning of the court difficult to understand. To me, Section 12 has a clear purpose and meaning: that people who had a child before they transitioned legally remain mother or father on the birth certificate of their child. It was not, as the judge found, intended to create an exception to the GRC so that trans parents are registered according to their gender assigned at birth.

For most people, being recorded on the birth certificate as mother and father reflects their gender and their relationship set-up. For cis men and women and most heterosexual couples, this is their de facto situation, that one person is mother and the other person is father, and the law has been set up to reflect this. But now that queer people can and do have children openly, our lives brush up against the law to show how the law and the courts are yet to catch up with our reality.

Freddy McConnell has been a vocal advocate on this point. He has argued that Section 12 was meant to reassure legislators that trans people would continue to be responsible parents to their children and that the lawmakers did not consider that trans people might have children after they transitioned. In evidence to parliament, he explained:

> we know that trans people were expected, if not legally forced, to 'fully transition', which in turn would prevent them becoming biological parents. We know that transition was, and sometimes still is, seen as a one-size-fits-all linear process. We know that doctors did not understand the effects of testosterone

on trans male fertility, i.e. that it causes no damage. The possibility of post-GRC biological parenthood was not just ignored, it was unthinkable.

Freddy McConnell is a man. He has been able to change his own birth certificate, but he is mother on his son's birth certificate. He did not give birth as a mother and then change this legal gender. His was a situation in which the law already recognised him as a man. The judge's decision had the effect of reinstating his previously assigned gender, albeit by arguing that 'mother' is now a gender-neutral term.

In court, the judge had heard independent evidence from an expert appointed to consider the best interests of the child, YY. The expert explained:

> As to the contents of the birth certificate, in my view it is important for YY's identity and self-esteem that his birth certificate reflects the reality of his life. The person who gave birth to him was and is male. 'Father' means 'male parent'. That is exactly what TT [McConnell] is. The birth certificate could reflect this reality by either listing TT as 'father' or 'parent'. Anything else gives the impression of something secretive or shameful. This could lead YY to feeling excluded from society and that he is different or odd.
>
> I note that YY's birth certificate will only have one parent listed, which will inevitably invite questions about the 'missing' parent. Although lots of children do not have a father listed, a missing mother is currently unusual and this may well be picked up on. However,

if TT is listed as 'mother', the questions are likely to be even more intrusive given that T is clearly a male name. This would cause YY distress and again give rise to feelings of being different.

The expert was clear that registering McConnell as 'mother' would 'put him back to square one in his fight for recognition as a man'. McConnell has said of the judgment that if gender recognition is revoked at the point of parenthood, then 'trans people must informally agree to not reproduce to be legally recognised. What is this if not de facto sterilisation?'

McConnell challenged the initial decision in the Court of Appeal. The case was heard by three judges, including the Lord Chief Justice of England and Wales. The court found that the Registrar General for England and Wales was correct to register Freddy McConnell as the mother of his child. The court accepted that for a trans man, being named as mother on a birth certificate is a 'significant interference with a person's sense of their own identity' given that the relationship is actually one of father and son. However, the court held that the interference with his rights was justified. The court found that there were two main reasons to legitimise why trans men should be named as mothers on a birth certificate. One reason was bureaucratic: to ensure the maintenance of a clear and coherent scheme of registration of births. The other reason was the rights of the child, including the right to know who gave birth to them and what the person's legal status is. In the UK, a person who gives birth — that is, the mother — has automatic parental responsibility from the moment of birth. This is not the case for the father.

As *The Guardian* commented, 'In the appeal court, Lord Burnett came down in favour of the right of a child born to a transgender parent to know the biological reality of its birth, rather than the parent's right to be recognised on the birth certificate in their legal gender.' The court placed an emphasis on the child knowing its origins, but McConnell's case dealt with this point. He argued that he could have been registered as the gestational parent or birth parent. This would have allowed his son to know the biological reality of the birth while also allowing McConnell to keep his name and not be registered as mother.

What objections can there be to having a term such as 'gestational parent' or 'birth parent' on a birth certificate for the very few trans and non-binary folks who give birth? The court's analysis is tantamount to saying: *listen, being called 'mother' on the birth certificate is not that bad.* There is no deep analysis of what it means for a trans person to be misgendered or of the hurt it may cause both father and child to see the parent named as a mother after the bravery of a transition.

Parents should not be reduced to their procreative functions. G, the mother of my child is just as much a 'mother' as I am, and I say that as the person who gave birth. This is my example, but there are so many I can give. Too many courts are falling into a trap of biological essentialism, which undermines all kinds of queer family and kinship structures and broader feminist struggles for women's self-determination, never mind the self-determination of trans people. Really, there is no reason in law why Freddy McConnell or someone like me cannot be registered as father, and our female partners (if we have them) registered as mother, regardless of who gives birth. And if birth origins are really the main consideration, then words like 'gestational parent' or 'gestational person' can be used as a marker. Mother is not always the person who gives birth. Sometimes dads give birth too.

However, as McConnell's case and similar decisions show, the law is yet to catch up with this reality.

McConnell's case is not the only one that shows the difficulties trans men have when their lives brush up against the law. In the US, Thomas Beatie made headlines around the world when he became pregnant and gave birth to a child in 2008. He was known as America's first 'pregnant father'. *The New York Times* commented on the case in the following terms:

> That this story attracted attention around the world was hardly surprising. Who, after all, could resist the image of a shirtless Madonna, with a ripe belly on a body lacking breasts and with a square jaw unmistakably fringed by a beard?

The article describes the story as 'partly a carnival sideshow and partly a glimpse at shifting sexual tectonics'. I would hope now, 15 years later, that we are past the freak-show narrative and that trans parenting is more normalised. Beatie had three children with his wife during their relationship, but in 2012 they decided to divorce. What should have been a simple process turned into a legal quagmire. The couple had married in Oregon, which legally recognised him as a man. Same-sex marriage was not yet available across the US. But when they came to divorce, a judge denied their divorce petition, on the grounds that Arizona, where they lived, did not recognise same-sex marriage. Because Beatie still had reproductive capacity to give birth to children, the judge found that he was a woman. Therefore, it was a same-sex marriage.

The Transgender Law Center intervened in the case with an amicus brief, calling out the dangers of the legal reasoning of the judge:

> if [the law] is interpreted to require transsexual individuals not only to undergo irreversible medical treatment to physically transition into their new sex, but also to be sterilized and forego forever the opportunity to bear biological children, it would unconstitutionally infringe upon the most-fundamental of rights.

Those most fundamental rights include our rights to bodily autonomy, sexual and reproductive rights, and our rights not to be tortured. Many countries and courts are having a problem understanding that trans and genderqueer people have children. That trans people can give birth and be parents. The sad fact is that in many countries trans people are sterilised to prevent us from having children.

There is a long history of sterilising trans people and women. This is a form of gender-based violence. Throughout the 19th and 20th centuries, countries used surgical sterilisation as a permanent method of birth control. Forced or coerced sterilisation has been used against Romani women in Slovakia and the Czech Republic. It was used extensively by the Nazis in Germany against a wide range of social groups, including unmarried mothers, ethnic minorities, prostitutes, and gender-nonconforming people; an estimated 400,000 people were sterilised. More than 270,000 women were forcibly sterilised in Peru as part of a government-run birth-control programme up until the year 2000. In 2020, the BBC reported that China is forcing Uyghur women to be sterilised.

While sterilising women is now rightly recognised as a form of violence against women, many countries around the world continue to have laws that require trans people to be sterilised before they are able to legally transition. In some countries, there is no provision for official legal recognition for trans people. But in countries where there is legal recognition, some impose completely unjustified provisions such as forced divorce and forced sterilisation.

In 1972, Sweden became the first European country to recognise trans people and their affirmed gender. But it came at a price for trans people: they had to prove that they were unable to reproduce, which often meant they had to submit to sterilisation. The idea of trans men becoming pregnant was seen as farcical, comical, or monstrous.

In 2017, 22 out of the 41 countries in the Council of Europe that recognised a trans person's identity also enforced a sterilisation requirement in law. These laws include provisions for the 'disabling of reproductive function' and the 'removal of sexual organs and mammary glands' before trans people can be recognised in national legal systems. Many trans people in Europe have found themselves in a legal limbo when such surgery is unavailable, unaffordable, inaccessible, or unwanted.

It was only recently that the European Court of Human Rights made it clear that sterilising trans people is contrary to our human rights. While teenagers across the world were listening to Justin Bieber telling everyone to 'Love Yourself', governments across Europe were still telling trans people to undergo surgery that would remove their reproductive capabilities. In 2017, three trans women — A.P, Émile Garçon, and Stéphane Nicot — created an important precedent. The women explained to the ECHR that the courts in France had denied them gender recognition unless they surgically altered their sexual anatomy, deeming hormone therapy and living as women insufficient to recognise them as women. The courts in France reasoned that recognising the women's gender without sterilisation surgery would create an unacceptable 'third gender', 'namely persons of female appearance who nevertheless continue to have a male external sexual anatomy but can marry a man … As the case-law currently stands, such a situation is wholly prohibited.'

I'm very happy to say that the ECHR found that France had violated the trans women's right to private life by making recognition of gender identity 'conditional on sterilisation surgery or on treatment which, on account of its nature and intensity, entailed a very high probability of sterility'. The court explained that sterilisation 'goes directly to individuals' physical integrity' and to a person's very existence, and that

French law at the time presented trans people with an 'impossible dilemma': undergo irreversible treatment against their wishes or forgo being able to have their gender identity recognised.

While the decision has been recognised as an important victory for trans rights, requiring Council of Europe states to end sterilisation and infertility requirements in the law, the case is disappointing. The court found that medical examinations or requiring individuals to prove a mental-health diagnosis do not breach the human rights of trans people. These requirements do breach our rights; there is no need for them. I am hopeful that the court's approach to trans rights will continue to evolve. A person should be able to have their gender recognised without invasive medical procedures. Many trans men do not want to undergo genital surgery before changing their gender. And there are trans men who want to keep their reproductive possibilities open. The law has no place imposing itself on trans people and ending their reproductive capacities.

In 2021, the ECHR decided a case in relation to two trans men from Romania who complained that they were unable to obtain documentation in relation to their male gender. The trans men brought the case after they had top surgery and hormone treatment but were told by Romanian authorities they had to have further surgery, which could result in their sterilisation, before they would be issued with new documentation. Once again, the court recognised that trans people faced an 'impossible dilemma' of choosing between the right to have their gender identity recognised and the right to their physical integrity — and that this violates our fundamental human rights.

Even more bizarrely, in some countries, trans people have to prove that they are unable to have children before they can start the medical transition process. This was the case in Türkiye. A trans man brought his case to the ECHR explaining that Türkiye had refused his application to gain access to gender-affirming treatment because he could get pregnant. The court reasoned that it 'fails to see why persons wishing to undergo gender reassignment surgery should have to demonstrate that they are unable to procreate even before the physical process of gender change can be undertaken'. The court found that the only way for the trans man to access gender-affirming treatment, including hormones, would have been to undergo a sterilisation operation and that 'due respect for his physical integrity precluded any obligation for him to undergo this type of treatment'.

As a human-rights lawyer, I can say that sterilisation and surgical requirements are contrary to international human-rights law. Trans and non-binary people should be able to access gender-affirming care on their own terms. To decide what treatment we want and what care we need. To live in the bodies that we want to live in, without state violence on our bodies. We should not be pathologised. Rather, states should offer us the care that we need as part of our right to health. It should also ensure that legal pathways for recognition are simple.

Legal models in Ireland and Spain have shown over the past few years that self-identification is workable and practical, as I discuss in the next chapter. A trans man who gives birth can be registered on a child's identity documents as a father of the child. The sky has not fallen down.

The legal fictions continue when it comes to intersex people. Intersex people are born with sex characteristics, reproductive organs, or hormonal patterns that do not fit into the typical binary of male or female bodies. They have always existed. Recent estimates suggest that 1.7 per cent of the world's population are born intersex. Intersex people have diverse gender identities and sexual orientation. They can be straight or gay and identify as man, woman, intersex, or non-binary. Sadly, intersex people are frequently subject to unnecessary surgical procedures in order to conform their bodies to binary stereotypes.

In 2015, an EU survey found that 21 of the 27 member states still carried out forced or coercive medical interventions on intersex children. Human-rights bodies — following advocacy by intersex people — have drawn attention to how these procedures violate a myriad of human rights. The procedures also have lifelong impacts on sexual and reproductive health; they can cause infertility, incontinence, and loss of sensation and pleasure, resulting in both mental and physical suffering.

International human-rights bodies have repeatedly told states that they must stop this form of surgery. They have called on states to 'take necessary measures to prohibit medically unnecessary gender confirmation surgery on intersex infants and children', and have made it clear that countries must ensure that there is an enabling environment for intersex children so that their physical integrity and preferred gender identity are respected. In recent years, concerns over unnecessary medical procedures on intersex children have been raised in relation to Germany, Denmark, Belgium, Czechia, Bulgaria, and others.

Intersex people also face a bureaucratic denial of their existence, with states forcing them to register as male or female even when this does not reflect their reality. Yet the law does not grasp, refuses to recognise, denies intersex people existence and creates absurd outcomes, such as designating intersex people with a gender against their will and lived experience.

In January 2023, the European Court of Human Rights decided a case brought by an intersex person identified in legal documents as Y. Y wanted France to recognise that they had been born intersex. As Y explained to the court, they had neither testicles nor ovaries, nor had they gone through puberty or ever produced sex hormones such as testosterone or oestrogen. Out in public, they were perceived as female, even though their birth certificate states that they are male. Y went to the ECHR seeking justice after the French courts refused to rectify the birth certificate and correct Y's gender. Y was 63 years of age; they had never thought of themselves as anything other than intersex.

The ECHR accepted that Y is a biologically intersex person. They also accepted this meant that Y's reality was not set out in the birth certificate. But despite the 'difficult situation in which intersex people find themselves in terms of the right to respect for private life, especially the discrepancy between the legal position and their biological reality', the court dismissed Y's case. The judgment recalls the work of law professor Dean Spade, written about trans people but equally applicable to intersex people: '[We] are told by the law, state agencies, private discriminators, and our families that we are impossible people who cannot exist, cannot be seen, cannot be classified, and cannot fit anywhere.' Y was not asking for a legal revolution, simply the legal acknowledgement of a fact: their intersex status. But in 2023, the highest human-rights court in Europe is still failing intersex individuals.

The way the law works to deny queer people their lived experiences involves an erasure of bodily realities and known identities. It involves the substitution of a heterosexist and heteronormative framework onto our lives. It involves the courts telling us that we exist only within a gendered binary, and that when we fall outside it, we just have to deal with it. There is still a long way to go to replace fiction with nonfiction.

In October 2022, I sat down for dinner with my colleague Jen Robinson. We were working on our last edits for our book and celebrated that night with sushi after we made our way through the final changes. Over the previous year or so, Jen and I had been speaking nearly every day, mostly about our book, but we had started to become close as friends. 'Tell me about you,' she said that night at dinner. 'When did you come out?'

After working together for nearly six years, I told her my coming-out story for the first time. I told her about my first crush, about lying on the floor of the church, about struggling with my sexuality in such a conservative setting. Then I told her something that I had not told many people about. That I'd been keeping inside. I told her that I was going to get top surgery.

I hadn't spoken to anyone else at work about this. I barely spoke to my friends about it. It felt so precious and vulnerable. I was worried about how she would react. I was worried about getting asked my preferred pronouns on a stage in front of 1,000 people in Sydney at our first book talk in a few weeks. I worried that I would get a negative reaction like the ones I've had since from some people who have asked why I have to mutilate myself. I need not have worried.

'I love you regardless of your gender,' she told me. And I knew then that I was ready to break free of the binary.

Chapter 8
I Am What I Am

Ireland was one of the first countries to allow trans people to self-declare their gender — the result of an 18-year legal battle by dentist Dr Lydia Foy, a trans woman who took on the Irish justice system. She started proceedings in 1997 and the first judgment in her favour was delivered on the 19 October 2007. I had just started my final year at Trinity after a year living in Paris. The radio was playing 'Umbrella' by Rihanna, which somehow never seemed to go away. We were still listening to CDs. The only decoration on the walls of our student residence was, very sadly, a huge homemade poster of important case law that we needed to remember for our exams.

The *Foy* judgment was important not only because it was about trans rights, but also because it was the first time an Irish court had made a declaration of incompatibility, recognising that Irish law was out of step with the European Convention on Human Rights. This mechanism, which also exists in the UK, is used by judges to highlight to the government that a law fails to comply with human rights. The judges cannot strike down the law, so they refer it to government, making clear that it's out of step.

The judgment was drafted by Justice William McKechnie, then a High Court judge. He later moved to the Supreme Court until his retirement in 2021. The last four paragraphs of the 2007 judgment have particularly stayed in my mind. The High Court recognised that many trans people 'live in the opposite sex without any treatment', while others have hormonal treatment, and 'a small but very definite number cannot stop there.' A small minority of people — including Lydia Foy — have surgical procedures to confirm their gender. 'This is frequently undertaken at great personal cost, but notwithstanding this, virtually all would say that such sacrifices are inescapably worth it.'

McKechnie understood that there is a spectrum within the trans community and different ways of living in and across the binary, from living in the 'acquired gender' without any form of medical intervention, to undergoing surgical procedures. Concluding the judgment, the judge noted the suffering and plight of trans people who had tried to change their legal identity in Ireland:

> Those at the forefront of such a quest many years ago, faced a public and a legal system which was much less sympathetic and much less understanding than hopefully what it is today. Everyone as a member of society has the right to human dignity, and with individual personalities, has the right to develop his being as he

sees fit; subject only to the most minimal of State interference being essential for the convergence of the common good. Together with human freedom, a person, subject to the acquired rights of others, should be free to shape his personality in the way best suited to his person and to his life. All persons by virtue of their being are so entitled.

It took time and further legal action from Foy, but the High Court's decision ultimately led to the enactment of the *Gender Recognition Act 2015*.

The Irish example shows that self-declaring gender identity through a simple administrative procedure is a viable, functioning model.

While some of the language of the 2007 judgment is now outdated, I remember feeling relief that Foy's journey for legal recognition had reached a positive outcome and that Ireland was applying its human-rights obligations in its national judgments. I also remember thinking that her journey and struggle would have been too much for me. The trans people I had met in Dublin had told me of being shunned by their families and finding it difficult to get a job. I had my sights set on being a barrister and was scared that I wouldn't be able to have a career if I came out as trans. Being a lesbian was one thing; being trans felt like quite another. It wasn't until many years later that I met another trans barrister, heard their story of acceptance, and felt brave enough to follow my own path.

The sad fact is that there are no binding international human-rights standards specifically protecting trans rights. However, the Inter-American Court of Human Rights has started to issue progressive and humane jurisprudence showing how existing human-rights norms can be interpreted to be trans inclusive. The leading trans rights case at the time of writing was handed down by the Inter-American Court in 2021 and is called *Hernández v Honduras*. I must here place a warning because the facts of this case includes graphic physical and sexual violence.

Vicky Hernández, a 26-year-old trans woman, was brutally murdered on 28 June 2009. Vicky was a sex worker and activist. She lived with her family in San Pedro Sula, the second-largest city in Honduras, and faced high levels of violence for being a visible trans woman. Just two months before she was murdered, she went to the police to report that she had been attacked with a machete. The police told her 'that for all they cared, she could die'. Then, only a few weeks later, as a national curfew came into place, Vicky was found dead on the street. She was registered by the police as 'John Doe' and the cause of her death was recorded as a bullet wound. They found a condom close to her body. Two trans women who had also been working on the streets with her that night and who had been the last to see Vicky alive were murdered a few weeks later. Each was registered as male since there is no gender identity law in Honduras.

The Inter-American Court heard evidence that Honduras is a country where there is a high rate of violence and discrimination against the LGBTQ+ community. Various UN entities and courts have noted the high rate of crimes and human-rights violations faced by LGBTQ+ people generally and trans women particularly. In only a seven-month period in 2009–2010, 15 trans women and 14 gay men died violently. Many of the trans women murdered were less than 35 years old. Many were shot and left on the street. The court in Vicky's case heard evidence that some of the women were beaten, one was stoned, one stabbed, one run over, one burned, and one dismembered, castrated, and beheaded.

Even though Vicky had clearly been murdered, the police had not investigated. The court heard that her death formed a wider pattern of 'violence against the LGBTQ+ community' that is 'based on prejudices' and often linked to a desire to punish people who are seen as defying gender norms. The violence is not only against the individual who is attacked, but also a symbolic bloody message that queer people are not safe.

In Vicky's case, the court found that Honduras had violated a raft of her rights by failing to protect her and to investigate her death. Significantly, the court found that the rights to life, personal integrity, and gender identity are all closely related. The court explained that Vicky's murder must be understood in a context where the state had failed to provide trans people with the ability to have their right to dignity and identity recognised.

The court indicated that it is a right of each person to be able to define his or her sexual and gender identity autonomously, and that the information set out in official records and on identity documents 'should correspond to and coincide with their self-defined identity'. The court held that states must ensure everyone is able to register, change, rectify, and amend their name, photograph, and reference to sex or gender 'without interference by the public authorities or by third parties. This necessarily means that those who identify themselves with diverse gender identities must be recognized as such.' The court also held that the murder of Vicky Hernández was a form of gender-based violence against trans women. The court ordered the government to make a number of reparations, including amending the law to put in place a procedure to ensure that trans people can have their gender identity recognised.

Hernández v Honduras is an important example of a court recognising how a lack of respect for and recognition of gender identity can lead to a discriminatory and violent social context for trans people. But it should not take the brutal murder of trans women and widespread impunity over their deaths for change to happen on this issue. Especially since the Inter-American Court had already made it clear in an advisory opinion back in 2017 that states must respect and protect the right to dignity, including the intentions, aspirations, and life decisions of trans people. The court advised that under human-rights law it is for the individual to freely determine and self-identify their gender. It explained:

> gender identity has been defined as the internal and individual experience of gender as each person feels it, which may or may not correspond to the sex assigned at birth. This includes the personal experience of the body as well as other expressions of gender, such as dress, speech and mannerisms. Thus, for this Court, recognition of gender

identity is necessarily linked to the idea that sex and gender should be perceived as being a part of the constructed identity that is the result of the free and autonomous decision of each person, and without this having to be subject to their genitalia.

It is the subjective sense of self that is important, the court explained. The 'psychosocial sex should be given pre-eminence over the morphological sex in order to fully respect the right to sexual and gender identity'. The court found that a lack of recognition of gender or sexual identity 'could result in indirect censure of gender expressions that diverge from cisnormative or heteronormative standards'. The court explained that restrictions placed on people because of their gender identity are due to fears, stereotypes, and social and moral prejudices with 'no reasonable basis'.

The court calls on states to provide trans people with the full protection of all human rights. In order to comply with these rights, states should ensure that trans people have legal recognition of their gender. The states can choose the appropriate procedure to comply with these obligations but:

> (a) these should be centered on the complete rectification of the self-perceived gender identity; (b) these should be based solely on the free and informed consent of the applicant without involving requirements such as medical and/or psychological or other certifications that could be unreasonable or pathologizing; (c) these should be confidential, and

the changes, corrections or amendments to the records and on the identity documents should not reflect the changes made based on the gender identity; (d) these should be prompt and, insofar as possible, cost-free, and (e) these should not require evidence of surgery and/or hormonal therapy.

The Office of the United Nations High Commissioner for Human Rights has also affirmed the right of trans people to legal recognition of their gender identity and has confirmed that trans people should be able to change their gender in official documents without being subject to onerous or abusive requirements. The UN has noted that these rights are violated in all regions around the world and that failing to allow trans people to change their documents or to legally change genders puts people at risk of multiple human-rights violations, including rights to health, education, employment, accessing bathrooms, and freedom from violence.

The UN has set out a list of key laws and policies that countries should implement based on human-rights standards. It provides that legal recognition of gender identity should:

1. Be based on self-identification and self-determination.
2. Be based on a simple administrative process.
3. Impose no requirement of medical certification, diagnosis, sterilization, surgery, medical treatment, pathologization or divorce.
4. Recognise non-binary identities.
5. Ensure children have access to recognition of their gender identity.

It recommends access to healthcare including gender affirming procedures and treatments, and that governments should provide justice and compensation to trans people for past human-rights violations, such as legal requirements that led to sterilisation. Some countries have taken this on board. In 2020, it was reported that the Netherlands had agreed to pay 2,000 trans people 5,000 euros each in redress for forcing them to undergo sterilisation to legally change their gender. This followed the establishment of a Swedish scheme in 2018.

In March 2023, I went to see Paul B. Preciado perform his speech 'Can the Monster Speak?' in the Conde Duque theatre in Madrid. I'd been looking forward to it for months. The queue into the venue was full of queers of all descriptions. It felt like going to church, nearly a religious experience, a form of worship of a queer idol. The performance was based on Preciado's experience of trying to give a speech in Paris in 2019. The Spanish gender scholar had been jeered and laughed at by an audience of 3,500 psychoanalysts when he tried to speak about his own experiences of the gender binary and pathologisation as a trans man. He was unable to deliver his talk in the Palais de Congrès, but the incident caused a scandal, and he published his speech in a book, which he was now performing to audiences in Spain.

Reading from a podium, he told the silent room that 'the journey of gender transitioning, however tortuous and erratic it may appear, made it possible for me to experience life beyond these limits' — the limits to our ways of feeling and loving. He told us that there is beauty beyond the gender binary. I needed to hear his words that night. To hear the affirmation of my own views represented on stage: that transition can be a way out of the binary, an act of resistance, a part of my feminist politics and my political and personal decision to live my life the way I want. Due to Preciado's activism, and the activism of many others over the decades, I was now on my own journey and able to shape my path in, nearly, my own terms. Preciado finished his reading to a standing ovation. Tears of joy silently streamed down my face at the applause.

He was speaking at a historic moment in Madrid. Only weeks before, on 16 February 2023, Spain had passed two laws in the same day: a law on abortion; and a law on gender recognition, called the *Ley Trans*. The *Ley Trans* allows people to self-declare their gender — as in several other countries in the world, it does not require a diagnosis of gender dysphoria. It also bans conversion-therapy practices and surgery on intersex babies, and allows for equal parental rights for lesbian mothers. The law officially came into force on 2 March 2023. A Spanish national who is trans can now change the gender on their official documents without undergoing two years of hormonal treatment or other medicalisation. Children as young as 16 can self-declare their own gender under the law, with the then secretary for state Ángela Rodríguez Martínez, known as Pam, explaining that 'At 16 people can work, have sexual relations, abort — they should also be able to choose their gender.'

The change in the law in Spain had a direct impact on my decision to start the process of obtaining gender-affirming care. I had decided some years before the change in the law that I was ready to change the course of my gender journey, but I was adamant that I did not want to go through the gender-recognition process as it is in the UK. I did not want to go before a board of strangers to justify decisions concerning my own gender. I also did not want medical professionals to dictate to me how my gender journey had to look and how it had to be. I did not want to be forced to change my name, live in an acquired gender for two years (whatever that means), and take hormones for two years before a doctor or clinic determined that I was eligible for surgery. I wanted control over my own body.

As Lady Hale explained in the Supreme Court case concerning the Northern Irish prohibition of abortion, 'The starting point for any discussion of the legal issues has to be the right of all human beings, male and female, to decide what shall be done with their own bodies.' While this is a long-standing principle of the common law, it is not reflected in practice in the UK. But in Spain, and other countries such as Ireland, changes means that trans people do not need a diagnosis of gender dysphoria anymore to get top surgery or gender-affirming care. We can increasingly decide what to do with our own bodies (if we have the means to pay for it or can wait for the care that we need).

Paul B. Preciado has long argued that nothing justifies the state's acting as a guarantor of sex changes but not of other surgeries such as breast enlargement or a nose job. He calls for trans people to be the author of their own journeys and destinies without legal, political, and biological specifications of what trans people should look like, of what they can and cannot do with their bodies. The legal and medical controls that regulate gender-affirming care are not merely administrative in nature; they can leave trans people open to criminalisation. In England and Wales, the *Misuse of Drugs Act 1971* was amended in 1996 to include testosterone on the list of controlled substances. Supplying the hormone without a permit may incur a maximum penalty of 14 years imprisonment and a heavy fine. As the poet Harry Josephine Giles notes in the poem 'May a Transsexual Hear a Bird?', it would be a criminal offence 'to give to my friend'. Gender piracy or gender hacking is prohibited.

The change in the law in Spain followed a move by the World Health Organization in 2019 to end the categorisation of being trans as a mental and behavioural disorder. The UN welcomed this move, calling the pathologisation of trans people 'stigmatising' and a 'scientifically unfounded classification'. Experts at the UN noted that 'pathologisation has historically been, and continues to be, one of the root causes of human rights violations against persons who identify as trans or gender diverse.' The revision of the International Classification of Disease (ICD-11) by the WHO means that countries should now review their medical classifications and adopt measures to allow for legal gender recognition and to provide gender-affirming healthcare.

The 'debate' on trans rights occurs around a number of flashpoints. These relate to the regulation of single-sex spaces, sport, bathrooms, detention facilities, and puberty blockers for trans children. Most of these issues have been used to justify the retention of the current pathologising model, quashing proposals and changes that would allow for self-declaration and self-determination over gender. Some argue that a change in the model would lead to an encroachment on women's rights, leading to greater violence against women in single-sex spaces such as prisons and bathrooms.

I understand the work that feminists have put in for decades setting up rape crisis centres and fighting for women's spaces so that they can be safe. I have worked in many legal forums for the elimination of discrimination against women. Violence against women is endemic, pervasive, the most common human-rights violation in the world. One in three women have experienced gender-based violence. Anyone who has lived in a woman's body can attest to the fear and danger of male violence. But concerns about this violence in arguments over trans self-determination is misplaced. The citing of an exception should never dictate the rule. That some people commit benefit fraud does not mean that we should scrap the welfare state. That some women attack other women in prison does not lead to calls for the abolition of women's prisons. That Karen White, a trans sex offender, assaulted women while on remand at HMP New Hall, a woman's prison in England, does not mean that trans women are predators or a danger to women.

In March 2023, after I went to see Paul B. Preciado, I was invited to the elite American university Yale to speak on a panel with radical feminist law professor Catharine A. MacKinnon. The mother of feminist legal theory was acerbic in her rejection of the biological essentialism of 'gender-critical' feminism and explained why feminist politics must be inclusive of those who identify as women. She dismissed arguments that self-declaration of gender would allow sexual predators to use this mechanism to abuse women in prisons. 'Sexual abuse in prisons is systematically and institutionally normalised,' she orated, pointing out that the primary threat to women in prison is by prison guards, mainly men. Sitting beside me, MacKinnon noted how trans women are more likely to be attacked in women's bathrooms than pose a danger in those spaces. She cautioned feminists against adopting a stance that runs counter to trans rights and the rights of trans women:

> It turns out, nature is fragile, much easier to change than society. Over the last 50 years, humans have changed the weather without even trying, while male dominance, despite massive effort, has barely budged.

The enemy of feminism is male violence, male gendered oppression of women, the patriarchy, not trans people or human-rights-compliant models of self-determination.

The issues that are most talked about — bathrooms, detention facilities, sport — are not the issues that have the greatest impact on the lives of trans people. Homelessness, familial and societal stigma and rejection, the inability to access healthcare, pathologisation — these are the issues that should be talked about. These are the issues that show that trans people as a small percentage of the population continue to be disadvantaged and discriminated against in society. I have been told many times that trans people are a powerful lobby, silencing speech and perpetuating cancel culture. 'What trans people?' I respond. 'Who?' Give me the names of these incredibly powerful, influential trans billionaires, because I don't know them. Do you? How many cis people have met and spoken with a trans person about their lives? How often are trans voices really heard?

When I first told my friends in London about my gender journey as I call it, they were worried for me. People were worried not only that I might be lonely through the process, but also that I might be subject to discrimination and violence. This isn't surprising given that the vast majority of what we read about trans lives in the media is bleak and depressing. As Shon Faye and C.N. Lester have documented, trans people receive huge amounts of media scrutiny and attention in the UK, often in an extremely negative way. Lester has written about how trans people are often the butt of the joke, marked out as strange, and how trans people are portrayed in UK tabloids as 'confused, deceitful, delusional, damaged, predatory, brave (sometimes), pitiable, pathetic. A punchline, a warning, a mistake.' Faye has argued that portrayal of trans people in the tabloids has moved from them being depicted as 'freak shows' to something to be feared. Trans folks are portrayed as proponents of a new gender ideology, fair game to be attacked in the media and online.

The 2021 UK census, published in January 2023, found that in England and Wales only 0.5 per cent of the adult population reported that the gender they identify with was not the same as their sex registered at birth. This means that a tiny proportion of the population receives an outsized proportion of negative media attention and public scorn on social media. It is no wonder that many trans people never come out of the closet.

Many accounts of trans men's lives that I have read or seen represented on screen have included stories of physical or sexual violence or abuse. Those accounts are important, but they require a balance too. Trans people live happy, ordinary, normal lives. We just rarely see those lives reflected around us. Trans people have communities, are in relationships, date. We are siblings, children, and parents. We are lawyers, doctors, the deputy prime minister of a small European country (yes, Belgium, from 2020 to 2024), the head of research institutes, judges, plumbers, singers, actors, Buddhist monks. We are all different and really may not have much in common other than our desire to live our lives beyond the gender assigned to us at birth. Or as Travis Alabanza puts it, 'Wanting more possibilities than the one you forced on me.' I am constantly learning from a younger generation about their views on gender identity and diversity, and why the law has to catch up to reflect these lived realities. My story is simply one story and one experience. But I share it here because our own voices are rarely heard above the cacophony of the 'trans debate'.

As some of the most powerful figures in the world take to their huge platforms to malign trans people, I feel it my duty to advocate for trans rights. As a human-rights lawyer and as someone on a gender journey, I know that trans people should not have to fear coming out. We should not fear being unable to access the healthcare that we need. We should not have to go through arduous administrative procedures to have our gender recognised. We should not be subject to what the trans law professor Dean Spade has called 'administrative violence'. We should not fear that the state will use our transness against us in unrelated aspects of our lives. We should not be persecuted, discriminated against, and publicly shamed online or in the media for refusing to live within the gender binary or failing to conform to the standards of the binary. The law should be there to protect us from all of this, not reinforce these prejudices.

In 2023, Victor Madrigal-Borloz, the UN Independent Expert on protection against violence and discrimination based on sexual orientation and gender identity, transmitted his report to the General Assembly, outlining how there are people and communities around the world who do not identify within binary frameworks or Western framings of gender. The experience of the kathoey (Thailand), bakla (the Philippines), fa'afafine (Samoa), leitī (Tonga), and many more show that the term 'LGBTQ+' does not capture the rich diversities of sexuality and gender that exist and have existed everywhere throughout history. Madrigal underlined examples of gender pluralism and gender fluidity in many indigenous cultures and communities prior to colonialism. His report talks about energies and spirituality before a strict binary system was imposed on colonised peoples and gender and sexual nonconformity were criminalised. The Independent Expert notes that 'Heteronormative views of sexuality instilled by colonial Powers were inextricably linked to racist characterizations of gender and sexuality'.

While some countries (like Austria, Canada, Denmark, Germany, Iceland, Malta, New Zealand, and Pakistan) have changed their laws to recognise non-binary status or an X marker on official documents, this change is yet to occur in other countries, even those with progressive trans legislation such as Ireland. In most countries, the process of legal recognition for trans people — where it exists — remains confined within and across the binary. However, for many gender-diverse people, legal recognition is simply non-existent.

The waiting game for legislative change is an administrative nightmare, especially where birth certificates or documents are issued by a country or place that does recognise non-binary gender. This is a real issue for people with X markers on their passports or who have already been recognised as non-binary. For example, in one recent case in the High Court in England and Wales, the judges heard that the applicant, Ryan Castellucci, does not identify as either male or female, and has changed their gender to non-binary in the State of California, where they were born. Castellucci sought to have a Gender Recognition Certificate issued in the UK, but the Gender Recognition Panel refused to issue one because the process in the UK only recognises binary gender. The High Court found that the panel was correct: the concept of gender in UK law is binary, and the Panel has no power to issue someone with a non-binary certificate. It is for parliament to make such a change. The court dismissed Castellucci's challenge, meaning that they are a non-binary person in California but not in the UK, at least for the purposes of official documentation.

In 2016, the *Transgender Equality* report by the Women and Equalities Committee recommended that the UK introduce an option to record an individual's gender as X on a passport, and that the government should consider a legal category for individuals with a gender identity 'outside that which is binary and the full implications of this'. The matter of such passports came before the Supreme Court in *R (Elan Cane) v Home Secretary* in 2021. The court found that 'the degree of prejudice to the appellant which is attributable to the unavailability of an "X" passport' wasn't comparable to that suffered by previous trans applicants, such as in *Goodwin v United Kingdom*. The court noted that the appellant had never been harassed at a border and that 'Perhaps most importantly, there is not the obvious discrepancy between the appellant's physical appearance and the "F" marker in the appellant's passport'. The court held that even though the appellant had gender-affirming surgery, including a hysterectomy:

> the appellant has not undergone gender reassignment surgery, but a procedure which is undergone by many women, without any alteration to their gender ... Nevertheless, it can fairly be said that the appellant is in a different position from women who undergo

hysterectomies for the usual medical reasons, since the appellant was provided with a hysterectomy, at public expense, in order to alleviate the psychological distress resulting from identifying as non-gendered while possessing a woman's reproductive physiology. In those circumstances, it might be argued that it would be logical for the Government to accord recognition to the applicant's nongendered identity in the context of passports, as the NHS did in the context of medical treatment. There appear to me to be two flaws in the argument. First, the NHS did not recognise the applicant as being a non-gendered person: what it recognised was that the applicant was suffering from the medical condition of gender dysphoria, and it provided medical treatment to alleviate that condition. Secondly, the fact that the Government, through its funding of the NHS, bore the cost of the appellant's medical treatment does not logically entail that it should in addition bear the far greater costs which would be involved in introducing 'X' passports, or accept the other disadvantages ...

This logic is so flawed that it is hard to know where to begin to pick it apart. The appellant clearly had gender-affirming surgery. And even if they hadn't, the European Court of Human Rights since *Goodwin* has made it clear that surgery is not a requirement for legal recognition of a binary trans status. The fact that someone has had gender-affirming surgery is to me one important aspect of understanding how non-gendered and non-binary people in all their diversity hold their status and control of their bodies to be a fundamental part of their life scripts and self-determination. The Supreme Court placed weight on the issue of national security (in confirming identity), costs to the changes in the administrative system, and coherence of the administrative and legal practices within the domestic system to dismiss the claimant's own sense of their life. Lord Robert Reed, writing for the unanimous court, says, *your situation isn't too bad, you still look like a woman*. What if instead he asked a different question? What if he asked how the law could make the person's life more liveable, humane, beautiful, and included?

As Dr Victoria McCloud, the first trans judge in the UK, has explained:

> It is a complex world and I suggest that the evolutionary progress humanity has made and is making in fields such as technology, medicine, and the arts is in part fuelled by the greater participation of people, expressing their true identities, ideas, and selves in society, freed more than before from the constraints of previous eras.

McCloud has explained that the law at times 'struggles to keep up with society's gradual appreciation of the complexity of human life'. It was her words I thought of when I read Lord Reed's judgment. That as humans we are all possible variations and permutations, but the law and sometimes its judges would like to keep us in a binary box.

Australia changed its laws to allow an X marker on the passport in 2013. The introduction of the X marker has not led to chaos, uncertainty, or catastrophe. The government website explains that while Australia recognises the gender marker, not all countries do, and this may cause difficulties for gender-diverse passport holders. The problem isn't Australia; it's most of the rest of the world. It remains unclear to me why bureaucratic certainty and an upholding of the binary remains the priority of states when they really care so little about gender equality in their legal and social policy.

In fact, I am constantly baffled as to why strangers, mainly companies, want to know about my gender. I book train tickets; it asks for my gender. I book a plane ticket; it asks for my gender. I open a bank account; gender. We live in societies where we are asked to tick boxes male or female so often that we have naturalised the existence of these questions in our everyday lives. These requests for gender declarations and gender reveals. In most of the forms that I fill out, my sex or gender is absolutely irrelevant to the daily activity I am carrying out.

In countries like France and Germany, there has been a wave of litigation that seeks to draw attention to this gender bureaucracy. In France, an organisation called Mousse has become fed up with this situation and launched a legal case before the European Court of Justice. The court has been asked to consider whether France's national state-owned railway company, SNCF, violated European Union law by forcing passengers to choose between the titles 'Mr' or 'Ms' when buying their train tickets. The 64 individuals in the legal challenge complained that there was no non-binary option to choose from, and that the collection of such data is unnecessary and inaccurate, thus a breach of data protection laws. The applicants' lawyer Étienne Deshoulières explained:

> This procedure is not only a fight against outdated forms, but a battle for the recognition and respect of each individual in their singularity. It defends the right of every person not to be trapped in the gender binary that does not correspond to their true identity. It is a question of respect for fundamental rights to self-determination, non-discrimination and the protection of personal data.

This case is one of the first to challenge the compulsory collection of gender status. Why does a train company need to know our gender(s)? It's one of a new set of exciting legal developments seeking to break open those binary boxes.

At the beginning of this book, I called for a queer manifestation. For a world in which the law affirms our queer lives on our own terms and not in comparison with heterosexuality or the binary. Queer people around the world have been agitating for change, for recognition, for simple existence. The law is meant to value accuracy, dignity, bodily autonomy, and a whole range of human rights, but too often we see these sacrificed at the altars of consistency, control, certainty, and prejudice.

When Victoria McCloud gave her 'Rainbow Lives, Monochrome Laws' lecture at Queen's University Belfast back in 2018, she started with the word *prejudice*: 'Literally, of course, it is pre-judgement,' she explained, 'the application of rules or beliefs without proper or fair consideration. Typically, this takes the form of rigid decision-making informed by presumptions or superstitions rather than balanced evidence.' She then went on to explain that the law is a 'body of rights and obligations', a legal system, which has as its lifeblood and immune system, courts and professionals, through which 'it is possible to rid the body of the disease of prejudice, hatred, and oppression.' She asserted, 'If we bring the colours of the Rainbow into the law library and the legal profession and the judicial Bench, the greys and blacks of the law take on the brightest and most hopeful shades.'

I too — like Dr McCloud, like the Supreme Court of India, like so many progressive judges, LGBTQ+ activists, and human-rights lawyers — believe in the lifeblood of the law, its potential to be a living, breathing, curious, and creative mechanism that understands and celebrates the range of our human diversity. I work towards the realisation of a law that will allow queer people to live their own life scripts in balance with the rest of our heterosexual and cisgendered friends, siblings, and family members. We must call out the injustices and prejudices and continue to breathe life into the law.

It can change just as I have even during the years over which I wrote this book.

It is 2024. I am 38 years old and back in Holywood, Northern Ireland, staying just up the road from where I grew up. It's a stunning day for home. The sun is shining and I'm taking my kid down to play in Seapark. We pack up into the car, my girlfriend, her kid, my friend Spruce, and head along the road that took me to school every morning. When we pull into the park, the kids run towards the shoreline. I love this view of the Lough from the path that I walked along so many times in my tortured youth, agonising over my crushed hopes of young queer love.

I'm staring out over the water to Carrickfergus when my reverie is broken by Spruce, a hot brainy butch. She starts to tease me about my description of Holywood that she's been hearing for the past 20 years. The lack of diversity. 'I thought you were one of the only Asians in your school,' she says. 'It's true,' I respond, kind of unsurely, because looking around in Seapark today it's hard to believe. There is so much diversity, which simply was not the case when I was growing up here. Northern Ireland has come a long way. But then again, so have I since I first came out at 15 and realised that I was in love with a girl.

Standing in Seapark, I watch two young women go past wearing bikinis. It's not the weather or really the place for it, but it's brat girl summer, so they are on theme. I smile because I finally know what it feels like to want to walk around a beach (really a park) in swimwear.

Last summer, I agonised over what to wear when I went away with friends to a villa in Spain. I fancied the woman who invited me and suspected that she liked me too. I told her that I was trans. Now what was I going to do? I am a trans man, but I didn't have a man's body yet. What would I wear at the beach or at the pool? I didn't really need to worry about what she thought, because she accepted my masculinity from the moment we met and understood the journey that I was on. But I found summer a difficult time to negotiate. I wore sports T-shirts as I jumped into the swimming pool. I tried to cover my chest. I was awkward in myself and in my body. It was excruciating.

This summer is a totally different story. By the time Easter came around, I was happily pulling my shirt off and running into the sea. I didn't care if other people saw or remarked on my scars. My chest is my own special creation. I am free in my body. In the terms of Paul B. Preciado, I have found my 'way out of the regime of sexual difference'. The first time I ran into the sea in my swimming trunks, I properly understood the term *trans joy*. It has not left me since.

The night before our trip to Seapark, I turned to my girlfriend to tell her about my coming-out story and first love. It's one of those conversations that happens in the early part of a relationship, when you start getting to know each other and discovering each other's pasts, to piece together the people you have become. I told her that I had been devastated at the loss of my opportunity to explore love in my school days, to even find out if my crush would have been interested in loving me back. I didn't know then that I would be, could be, so happy as I am now. The narrative that we were both sold as teenagers was that being gay would be lonely, that we might struggle to find acceptance and love. Once I started to tell my friends that I was on a new gender journey, I got a similar reaction from some people: they worried that I would be lonely.

'I wish my 15-year-old self could see me now,' I said to my girlfriend, whose head was resting on my masculine chest in a hotel room that looked like it was last decorated in the 1980s. 'I bet you do,' she laughed, while stroking my cheek.

I fell asleep that night thinking that I wish my younger self could know that I would be lying just up the road with the most beautiful woman in my arms. I wish my little self could know how I would grow up to feel like the luckiest man alive.

Conclusion

Oscar Wilde was on my mind as I wrote my last book and I have continued to think of him. The law has come a long way since his time, yet we still have a long way to go. My American friend has seen same-sex marriage come to the United States and I have seen the self-declaration of gender enabled in Ireland and Spain. But we still have a long way to queer the law.

Decriminalising same-sex intimacy is an essential first step to allow us to live our authentic queer lives, but we need more than that. As the US Supreme Court has explained, 'Outlaw to outcast may be a step forward, but it does not achieve the full promise of liberty' — and we deserve it all. We must denounce laws that contribute to the violence and discrimination queer people face in our day-to-day lives. Not only laws on homosexuality. Laws on 'debauchery', 'vagrancy', and sex work have all been used to target LGBTQ+ people. At least six countries in the world criminalise 'cross-dressing', which is specifically used to target trans people. In Kuwait, there is a law prohibiting the 'imitation of the opposite sex'.

A second step is to ensure that queer people have the right to control and make decisions about their own bodies and healthcare, free from coercion, discrimination, and even criminalisation. In the US, a whole raft of anti-LGBTQ+ legislation has been passed, including laws that restrict or ban gender-affirming care. Some of these laws even threaten prison time for medical professionals who provide care to young people.

Third, queer people must be able to express themselves, to exercise their rights to self-determination, association, and speech. In too many countries, there are laws that prohibit the 'promotion of homosexuality' and prevent LGBTQ+ advocacy. The equivalent of Section 28 and *Don't Say Gay* are proliferating.

Fourth, we must do more to protect rainbow families and to help them navigate the web of legal decisions and rules that impact having a baby and being a queer parent.

Fifth, we must fight for trans rights. The right to go from A to B. But also fight for those who seek the recognition of their liminal or non-binary status. We must really question why the law is so scared of gender fluidity.

Finally, we must move towards a conception of human rights that focuses less on the violations and harms that we suffer and more on freedom and self-fulfilment. This is slowly emerging through some of the cases that brave activists are bringing to courts around the world, such as the Supreme Court of India. But when we are fighting violence, discrimination, and criminalisation, it leaves many of us with little time to consider how we can dream and advocate for the other beautiful rights enshrined within human-rights law. The rights to justice and peace in the world, to have the opportunity to earn a livelihood through the work we choose, to decent living, a healthy environment, rest, leisure, reasonable working hours, and access to food. These are all examples of our human rights enshrined in international law that we could be busy thinking about and advocating for if LGBTQ+ people had basic freedoms and rights.

Since there is no binding LGBTQ+ rights treaty, the onus continues to be on LGBTQ+ activists and individuals to bring cases and fight in legal systems for these rights. We have had to bring our cases to international and regional courts and explain why basic rights such as the right to family life belong and apply to us.

Little by little, we have worked to queer the law. To breathe life into the constitutions and legal provisions that have denied us our rights. This living, breathing capacity for change is what gives me hope that we may all move openly in the world with the person that we love and in the clothes that we want to wear. That we may live our lives to the beat of our own drums and dictate our own scripts.

That we have the right to love who we choose with the full protections of the state.

Acknowledgements

Thank you to the team at Scribe, particularly to Simon Wright, Laura Ali, David Golding, and Laura Thomas. A huge thank you to my agent, Laura Macdougall at United Agents, for believing in this book from the beginning. For reading early chapters of the work, thank you to Dr Emma Spruce, Ciara Murphy, Alexandra Ordolis, Luke Clark, Borja Novoa, the American, and Sergio Waisman. Thank you to Madeleine Rees, Roberta Kaplan, and Aisling McNiffe for sharing their wisdom and experiences with me. Thank you to my colleague and friend Jen Robinson, who encouraged me to write my story; now go finish yours. To the family who raised me: Mum, Dad, Rie, Taiyo, thank you. My thanks and love to G and our child, who have allowed me to tell our story, and for being part of my life journey of being a parent. Finally, thank you to the poet who accompanied me throughout the writing of this book.

Notes

A Note from the Author on Language
BOOKS
Eve Kosofsky Sedgwick, *Tendencies*, Duke University Press, 1993

Prologue
BOOKS
Jennifer Robinson and Keina Yoshida, *How Many More Women?: exposing how the law silences women*, Allen & Unwin (Australia), 2022 / *Silenced Women: why the law fails women and how to fight back*, Octopus (UK), 2024
Joseph Bristow, *Oscar Wilde on Trial: the criminal proceedings, from arrest to imprisonment*, Yale University Press, 2023
Oscar Wilde, *De Profundis and Other Prison Writings*, Penguin Classics, 2013

REPORTS

Wolfenden Committee, *Report of the Departmental Committee on Homosexual Offences and Prostitution*, September 1957

Chapter 1: In Private

The title of this chapter is a riff on the song by Robyn, 'Love Kills', when she says 'there's a penalty for love crimes'. Below are the books and legal cases that form the backbone of this chapter. Cases are listed in the order that they are discussed in the chapter.

BOOKS

Adrienne Rich, 'Poem II' of 'Twenty-One Love Poems', *The Dream of a Common Language: Poems 1974–1977*, W.W. Norton, 2013

Jeanette Winterson, *Oranges Are Not the Only Fruit*, Vintage Classics, 2024

Ruadhán Mac Cormaic, *The Supreme Court: the judges, the decisions, the rifts and the rivalries that have shaped Ireland*, Penguin, 2017

REPORTS

Policy Department for Citizens' Rights and Constitutional Affairs, EU Parliament, *Conversion Practices on LGBT+ People*, July 2023

CASE LAW

Dudgeon v United Kingdom (application no. 7525/76) 22 October 1981

Norris v Attorney General (1983) IESC 3

Norris v Ireland (application no. 10581/83) 26 October 1988

Tingley v Ferguson, Docket 22-942, 9th Circuit, December 2023

Chapter 2: Are You Ready for Love?

ARTICLES AND BOOKS

Dale Carpenter, *Flagrant Conduct: the story of Lawrence v. Texas*, W.W. Norton, 2013

Dianne Otto (ed.), *Queering International Law: possibilities, alliances, complicities, risks*, Routledge, 2018

Rahul Rao, *Out of Time: the queer politics of postcoloniality*, Oxford University Press, 2020

Senthorun Raj and Peter Dunne (eds), *The Queer Outside in Law: recognising LGBTIQ people in the United Kingdom*, Palgrave Macmillan, 2021

Walt Whitman, 'I Sing the Body Electric', https://whitmanarchive.org/item/encyclopedia_entry9

REPORTS

Human Dignity Trust, *Breaking the Silence: criminalisation of lesbians and bisexual women and its impacts*, 2016, https://www.humandignitytrust.org/wp-content/uploads/resources/Breaking-the-Silence-Criminalisation-of-LB-Women-and-its-Impacts-FINAL.pdf

Human Rights Watch, *This Is Why We Become Activists: violence against lesbian, bisexual, and queer women and non-binary people*, 2023, https://www.hrw.org/sites/default/files/media_2023/02/global_lbq0223_web.pdf

CASE LAW

Toonen v Australia (1994) UN Doc CCPR/C/50/D/488/1992

Flamer-Caldera v Sri Lanka (2022) CEDAW/C/81/D/134/2018

Bowers v Hardwick (1986) 478 US 186

Lawrence v Texas (2003) 539 US 558

Navtej Singh Johar v Union of India (2016) Writ Petition (Criminal) No. 76

Dobbs v Jackson (2022) Supreme Court 597

Dausab v Minister of Justice (2024) NAHCMD 331

Chapter 3: Express Yourself

A list of the books seized in Operation Tiger is available on the Senate House Library website: https://exhibitions.london.ac.uk/s/seizedbooks/page/home

ARTICLES AND BOOKS

Alfred Douglas, 'Two Loves', https://poets.org/anthology/love-dare-not-speak-its-name

Geoffrey Robertson, *The Justice Game*, Vintage, 1999

Graham McKerrow, 'Saving Gay's the Word: the campaign to protect a bookshop and the right to import queer literature', in Leila Kassir and Richard Espley (eds), *Queer Between the Covers: histories of queer publishing and publishing queer voices*, University of London Press, 2021

James Kirkup, 'The Love That Dares to Speak Its Name', available online

Martina Gillen, 'The Policy of Promotion: the clash of rights in sex education law', *Northern Ireland Legal Quarterly* 53(1), 2002

Nigel Nicolson, *Portrait of a Marriage*, Weidenfeld and Nicolson, 1973

Paul Baker, *Outrageous!: the story of Section 28 and Britain's battle for LGBT education*, Reaktion Books, 2022

Virginia Woolf and Vita Sackville-West, *Love Letters*, Vintage Classics, 2021

REPORTS

Office of the United Nations High Commissioner for Human Rights, *A Compendium on Comprehensive Sexuality Education*, March 2023

CASES

Gathercole's Case (1838)
Whitehouse v Lemon (1979) AC 617
Lee v Ashers Baking Company Ltd and Others (2018) UKSC 49
Bull v Hall (2013) UKSC 73
Masterpiece Cakeshop v Colorado Civil Rights Commission (2018) 138 S Ct 1719
303 Creative v Elenis (2023) 21 S Ct 476
Bostock v Clayton County (2020)

Chapter 4: I Know a Place
BOOKS

Dale Carpenter, *Flagrant Conduct: the story of Lawrence v. Texas*, W.W. Norton, 2013

Jeanette Winterson, *Frankissstein*, Jonathan Cape, 2019
Jeremy Atherton Lin, *Gay Bar: why we went out*, Granta Books, 2022

REPORTS
ILGA-Europe, Rainbow Map, https://rainbowmap.ilga-europe.org/
UK Lesbian and Gay Immigration Group, *Missing the Mark: decision making on lesbian, gay (bisexual, trans and intersex) asylum claims*, September 2013

CASE LAW
Oganezova v Armenia (application no. 71367/12 and 72961/12) 17 May 2022
HJ and HT v Secretary of State for the Home Department (2010) UKSC 31
Hurley v Irish-American Gay, Lesbian, and Bisexual Group of Boston (1995) 515 US 557
Identoba v Georgia (application no. 73235/12) 12 May 2015
Women's Initiatives Supporting Group v Georgia (application nos 73204/13 and 74959/13) 16 December 2021
Sabalić v Croatia (application no. 50231/12) 14 January 2021
Berkman v Russia (application no. 46712/15) 1 December 2020

Chapter 5: Husbands and Wives
BOOKS
Constance Debré, *Love Me Tender*, Tuskar Rock, 2023
Susan Golombok, *We are Family: what really matters for parents and children*, Scribe, 2020

Roberta Kaplan, *Then Comes Marriage: how two women fought for and won equal dignity for all*, W.W. Norton, 2015

CASE LAW
Atala Riffo v Chile (2012) Series C. No. 239
X v Poland (application no. 20741/10) 16 September 2021
Advisory Opinion OC-24/17 Inter-American Court of Human Rights, Requested by Costa Rica, 24 November 2017
Orlandi v Italy (application no. 26431/12, 26742/12, 44057/12, 60088/12) 14 December 2017
Coman v General Inspectorate for Immigration and Ministry of the Interior (2018) C-673/16
Minister of Home Affairs v Fourie; Lesbian and Gay Equality Project v Minister of Home Affairs (2005) Cases CCT60/04, CCT10/05
Zappone v Revenue Commissioners (2006) IEHC 404
Hollingsworth v Perry (2013) 570 US 693
United States v Windsor (2013) 570 US 744
Obergefell v Hodges (2015) 576 US

Chapter 6: You're Having My Baby
ARTICLES AND BOOKS
Amrita Pande, 'Revisiting Surrogacy in India: domino effects of the ban', *Journal of Gender Studies* 30(4), 2020
Audre Lorde, 'Poetry Is Not a Luxury', *Your Silence Will Not Protect You: essays and poems*, Silver Press, 2017
Celine Heath, 'Government Announces Huge Shake-Up to NHS IVF Rules', *Women's Health*, 23 July 2022

Eleanor Noyce, 'Inaugural Women's Health Strategy to Tackle IVF Inequality Faced by LGBTQI Women', *DIVA*, 20 July 2022

Susan Golombok, *We are Family: what really matters for parents and children*, Scribe, 2020

CASE LAW

In the Matter of an Application by the Northern Ireland Human Rights Commission (2013) NICA 37

X v Austria (2013) (application no. 19010/07) 19 February 2013

SC and GP v Italy (2019) CESCR Committee, UN Doc. E/C.12/65/D/22/2017

VMA v Stolichna obshtina, rayon 'Pancharevo' (2021) Case-C490/20

Whittington Hospital NHS Trust v XX (2020) UKSC 14

Paradiso and Campanelli v Italy (application no. 25358/12) 24 January 2017

Mennesson v France (application no. 65192/11) 26 June 2014

H v United Kingdom (application no. 32185/20) 31 May 2022

Advisory Opinion Requested by the French Court of Cassation (Request No. P16-2018-001) 10 April 2019

D v France (application no. 11288/17) 16 July 2020

Fjölnisdóttir v Iceland (application no. 71552/17) 18 May 2021

DB v Switzerland (application nos 58817/15 and 58252/15) 22 November 2022

Chapter 7: Born This Way

This chapters focuses on the case of Freddy McConnell, who was originally known in legal documents as TT.

ARTICLES AND BOOKS

A.K. Summers, *Pregnant Butch: nine long months spent in drag*, Soft Skull Press, 2014

Daniela Alaattinoğlu, 'Forced sterilisation in the Istanbul Convention: remedies, intersectional discrimination and cis-exclusiveness', in Johanna Niemi, Lourdes Peroni, and Vladislava Stoyanova (eds), *International Law and Violence Against Women: Europe and the Istanbul Convention*, Routledge, 2020

Dean Spade, *Normal Life: administrative violence, critical trans politics, and the limits of law*, Duke University Press, 2015

Emma Parker, 'Male Pregnancy and Queer Utopia in Paul Magrs's *Could It Be Magic?*', *Textual Practice* 28(6), 2014

Peter Dunne, 'Transgender Sterilisation Requirements in Europe', Medical Law Review 25(4), 2017

REPORTS

European Union Agency for Fundamental Rights, *The Fundamental Rights Situation of Intersex People*, May 2015

House of Commons Women and Equalities Committee, *Reform of the Gender Recognition Act*, December 2021

CASE LAW

Goodwin v United Kingdom (application no. 28957/95) 11 July 2002

TT and YY v Registrar General (2019) EWHC 2384 (Fam) and on appeal (2020) EWCA Civ 559

R (on the application of C) v Secretary of State for Work and Pensions (2017) UKSC 72

K.H. and Others v Slovakia (application no. 32881/04) 28 April 2009

L v Lithuania (application no. 27527/03) 11 September 2007

A.P., Garçon, and Nicot v France (application nos 79885/12, 52471/13, and 52596/13) 6 April 2017

X and Y v Romania (application nos 2145/16 and 20607/16) 19 January 2021

Y.P. v Russia (application no. 43399/13) 20 September 2022

A.H. v Germany (application no. 7246/20) 4 April 2023

O.H. and G.H v Germany (application nos 53568/18 and 54741/18) 4 April 2023

Y v France (application no. 76888/17) 31 January 2023

Chapter 8: I Am What I Am
ARTICLES AND BOOKS

C.N. Lester, *Trans Like Me*, Virago Press, 2017

Catharine A. MacKinnon, 'A Feminist Defense of Transgender Sex Equality Rights', *Yale Journal of Law and Feminism* 34(2), 2023

Dean Spade, *Normal Life: administrative violence, critical trans politics, and the limits of law*, Duke University Press, 2015

Finn Mackay, *Female Masculinities and the Gender Wars*, Bloomsbury Academic, 2023

Harry Josephine Giles, 'May a Transsexual Hear a Bird?', in Mary Jean Chan and Andrew McMillan (eds), *100 Queer Poems*, Vintage, 2022

Jack Halberstam, *Trans: a quick and quirky account of gender variability*, University of California Press, 2018

Maggie Nelson, *The Argonauts*, Graywolf Press, 2016

Paul B. Preciado, *Can the Monster Speak?: report to an academy of psychoanalysts*, Fitzcarraldo Editions, 2020

Shon Faye, *The Transgender Issue*, Allen Lane, 2021

REPORTS

Council of Europe, *Human Rights and Gender Identity and Expression*, 2024, https://rm.coe.int/issue-paper-on-human-rights-and-gender-identity-and-expression-by-dunj/1680aed541

Victor Madrigal-Borloz, *Report of the Independent Expert on Protection Against Violence and Discrimination Based on Sexual Orientation and Gender Identity*, 2022

CASE LAW

In the matter of an application by the Northern Ireland Human Rights Commission for Judicial Review (Northern Ireland) (2018) UKSC 27

Vicky Hernández et al. v Honduras, Series 422, 26 March 2011

Advisory Opinion OC-24/17 Requested by Costa Rica, 24 November 2017

Foy v an T-Ard Chlaraitheoir and Others (2007) IEHC 470

R (Castelluci) v Gender Recognition Panel (2024) EWHC 54 (Admin)

R (on the application of Elan-Cane) v Home Secretary (2021) UKSC 56

Case C-394/23, Mousse: request for a preliminary ruling from the Conseil d'État (France) lodged on 28 June 2023, *Association Mousse v Commission nationale de l'informatique et des libertés (CNIL), SNCF Connect*